Seven Myths ABOUT Small Groups

How to Keep from Falling into Common Traps

DAN WILLIAMS

INTERVARSITY PRESS
DOWNERS GROVE, ILLINOIS 60515

InterVarsity Press is the book-publishing division of InterVarsity Christian Fellowship, a student movement active on campus at hundreds of universities, colleges and schools of nursing in the United States of America, and a member movement of the International Fellowship of Evangelical Students. For information about local and regional activities, write Public Relations Dept., InterVarsity Christian Fellowship, 6400 Schroeder Rd., P.O. Box 7895, Madison, WI 53707-7895.

All Scripture quotations, unless otherwise indicated, are from the Holy Bible, New International Version. Copyright © 1973, 1978, International Bible Society. Used by permission of Zondervan Bible Publishers.

Cover illustration: Merilee Harrald Pilz

Cartoons on p. 16 and p. 30 are taken from Amusing Grace © 1988 by Ed Koehler and used by permission of InterVarsity Press.

Cartoon on p. 42 is taken from It Came from Beneath the Pew © 1989 by Rob Suggs and used by permission of InterVarsity Press.

Cartoon on p. 58 is taken from Way Off the Church Wall © 1989 by Rob Portlock and used by permission of InterVarsity Press.

Cartoons on p. 70 and p. 82 are taken from Church Is Stranger than Fiction © 1990 by Mary Chambers and used by permission of InterVarsity Press.

Cartoon on p. 98 is taken from Off the Church Wall © 1987 by Rob Portlock and used by permission of InterVarsity Press.

ISBN 0-8308-1721-2

Printed in the United States of America ∞

Library of Congress Cataloging-in-Publication Data
Williams, Dan, 1957-
    Seven myths about small groups: how to keep from falling into
common traps/Dan Williams.
      p. cm.
    Includes bibliographical references.
    ISBN 0-8308-1721-2
    1. Small groups.   2. Church group work.   3. Leadership.
  I. Title.
  HM133.W5   1991
  302.3'4—dc20

91-14011
CIP

15	14	13	12	11	10	9	8	7	6	5	4	3	2	1
03	02	01	00	99	98	97	96	95	94	93	92	91		

*To my wife, Sharon, and kids,
Kaitlin, Erin and Dylan—
the small group that made
this book possible*

Introduction

Why another book on small groups? After all, InterVarsity Press has several in print already, and NavPress brought out several more last year alone. Lyman Coleman and Serendipity put out more stuff all the time. In fact, there have never been more published resources for and about small groups. And that is a good thing—for there never have been more groups around.

However, there have also never been more groups with problems. In spite of so many books, so many groups are still missing the point, still falling into some deadly traps, still buying into myths about group life. There clearly is still some work to be done.

That is not to say that the work has not already begun. The many excellent books on small groups do contain some of the key principles included in this book, but they are hidden in the midst of other matters. In other cases, the principles here are not found at all in other books. Here is the critical thing—ignoring any of these seven myths can be deadly for a group.

I have attempted to make the mythology clearcut in each case, breaking new ground and even overemphasizing where necessary. Here is what an early reviewer said about chapter one, "I can't say that I've ever seen an entire chapter of a book devoted to the necessity, timing and situations in which a small group should end." But, as you will see, the importance of group endings cannot be overstated. I believe that the same could be said about the other topics.

Small Group Principles

I believe that Christians should not stay in the same place as they mature, and that different phases of their discipleship need to be expressed in different types of groups.

The basic group in a church or parachurch setting is known by many different names—growth groups, cell groups, koinonia groups, and kinship groups. In this book we will use the term *nurture group* to describe this basic type of group. In fact, when you do ask most small groups why they exist, the answer generally focuses on nurture through Bible study, sharing and prayer. More rarely socializing, worship and outreach might be mentioned, but nurture is the dominant theme.

My guru of groups is Roberta Hestenes. She often presents an excellent lecture on the seven keys for healthy and growing groups. My problem is that I cannot remember seven things. So I have boiled the seven keys down into three C's. They are contracting, cycles and closed membership. For nurture groups, these three elements are all you need to ensure vitality. First, have a clear aim (contracted goals). Second, know how long you are going to go before you evaluate and re-aim (cycle duration). And third, know with whom you are going to fulfill the aim (membership plan).

Prior to a basic nurturing experience, a new Christian might be part of an orientation group or a discipleship Bible study. These are usually short-term and have a well-defined agenda and curriculum with little room for variation. After a nurture group, people might find themselves in a specialty group which emphasizes one or more components of group life over other components. For example, there are accountability groups (which emphasize exhortation), prayer groups (which emphasize intercession), and training groups (which emphasize learning). Very popular today are worship groups (which emphasize certain spiritual gifts) and ministry groups (which emphasize healing). A growing trend is toward short-term support groups for special needs like grief and codependency.

After these kinds of group experiences, a more mature Christian should graduate at some point into a mission group. These groups exist primarily to serve those outside of the group in some way, though in some cases the service takes place by inviting people into the group (for example, evangelistic Bible studies). In general, mission groups are the most demanding and stretching. They can be larger and last longer than other groups. Where other groups are the place of preparation, mission groups represent the cutting edge of kingdom advancement in the world. Nurture groups and most specialty groups are boot camp and hospital units; mission groups are platoons on patrol.

Who Is This Book For?

The audience intended for this book is both groups and their leaders, as well as program planners. Actually, I see very little distinction between groups and group leaders, for every member leads. So it would be better somehow to expose the content of this book to whole groups rather than just to the official group organizers.

There are five kinds of leadership expressed in and through groups.

Designated leadership refers to the position I call the "coordinator" or "facilitator." The designation is made by the group itself, or by the planners in the church or other organization. It should not be a self-designation. The service provided by the coordinator to the group is very important. But the greatest service that a coordinator can offer is to not be too threatened by leadership from other members, even leadership that is expressed initially in terms of "rebellion."

Coordinators should actually foster shared leadership by arranging *delegated* leaders from the earliest stage (hosts, prayer secretaries) and also by recognizing and affirming *differentiated* leadership expressed through various roles played out in the group process (encouragers, summarizers). Groups should not be afraid of this diversity of gifts, and the specialization into *defined* leadership positions that can result. Such definition goes way beyond Bible study leadership. Although members should not be put into straightjacketed portfolios, allowing them to concentrate on particular types of leadership (worship leader, pastoring) prepares them for their next group experience and the mature contribution they will make. The ultimate fruit of good groups is *dispersed* leadership, especially through mission groups.

Although the focus of the book will be on nurture groups in local churches, it will also have something to say to other Christian fellowships that have a small group structure. Additionally, mission groups will be dealt with in chapter seven. In the final analysis, it is impossible to tear apart the close relationship between individual groups and whole group programs. So the book will be useful to program planners and overseers as well; occasionally, some comments are explicitly directed their way. Much more will appear in my companion volume, *Seven Myths about Small Group Programs.*

Using This Book
In the process of isolating some mythological rocks which can wreck

the small group journey, a few key features emerge which bear comment:

1. Myths die hard. The task involves controversy and debate. I hope that the negative tone that sometimes comes through (a necessary by-product when attacking false ideas) does not put the reader off. Please don't shoot the messenger. I also paint a positive picture of what groups can mean in the lives of ordinary people.

Do some of my dogmatic statements need further qualification? Probably, but you won't find it here. This is because my aim was to stimulate fresh thought and provoke discussion, so I have made strong claims. I hope that readers will not, in turn, be too defensive, but instead merely amend and adapt where they see fit.

2. Myths are complicated. So they must be approached from a strong theoretical base and with careful analysis. I hope that the resulting argument does not distract from the main conclusions. Some of the detailed material is committed to the resources section at the end in order to not break the flow of the chapters.

3. Myths in group work are interrelated. You will find some overlap from chapter to chapter. The issue of group leadership, for example, is covered over two chapters (four and five), as are the topics of membership (two and three) and Bible study (five and six). In addition, certain basic concepts about groups come up again and again, especially contracting.

4. Debunking myths is based on experience. Myths about small groups become clear not so much from reading textbooks but rather from years of exposure to testimonies about the joys and tragedies of small groups (in campus clubs, churches, college courses, seminars and consultations). That is why you will find more references to experience than to published sources. However, further reading is suggested in an appendix.

I like playing chess. Learning the rules about how to play chess is one thing, but it really gets fun when you learn how to set traps and pitfalls for your opponent. Naturally, it is also important at some stage to learn how to recognize and avoid pitfalls. For example, do you know that you can be checkmated in two moves if you are playing white—and if you are really careless? If not, you better find out how this can happen and see that it doesn't. This is a book which teaches groups and group leaders how to avoid the pitfalls in the small group game.

CHAPTER 1

• • • • •

MYTH #1

Groups should
last
forever

*"Come on, guys, come on down. I don't know exactly what
you did, but you can't stay up in the steeple crying
'sanctuary' all your lives."*

I spent the first few months of my tenure as a small groups coordinator at a large urban church giving permission for leaders and groups to quit. If the elders had known what I was doing I might have been out of a job! But providing a doorway for groups to decease turned out to be some of the best work I ever did; it was compassionate surgery aimed at saving the group program.

Ending groups may seem like a funny place to start a book on small groups. However, as we shall see, when it comes to groups, endings have everything to do with beginnings. When groups do not plan to end from the very start, they usually last one year too long—and it can seem like a very long one year, discouraging, frustrating, draining. As a groups doctor, I have discovered that this is the most common diagnosis among sick groups. It often requires radical treatment. Preventative medicine is far less painful.

A Tale of Two Groups

Meet John's group. It has been going for eight years. Three original members are left, plus two folks who are recent additions. The two newcomers have only been showing up sporadically, which is irritating for those who have been committed over the long term. But they don't complain much, because they are afraid of scaring off the "new blood." In fact, the group has lost three other new people in the last year, while other original members left years ago.

John is tired, feeling burned-out from trying to keep the group going; he was hoping that one of these new people would take over the leadership this year. But that doesn't seem to be happening—so maybe the group should think about ending. But what would happen to their friendships, developed after so many hours of sharing, studying, fighting and praying? On the other hand, everyone seems so disinterested, even bored. Maybe he will suggest that the group end, even though the members have always resisted the idea in the past. Besides, the church keeps asking them to carry on, for the sake of all the people who need to be in a group.

Now meet Sally's group. It has been going for two-and-a-half years. They are in the middle of a mission project which has been key in drawing the ten members together and in bringing out individual gifts. Michael is in charge of the project. Three other people share the Bible study leadership, consulting each week with the worship leader. The group meets at Joy's house because she has a gift of hospitality. Sally keeps an eye on the whole show, including evaluating the group against the contract they had adopted for this phase of their life together (more on such group agreements can be found in Resource One).

The group is particularly excited right now, because their current contract includes a "volcano clause" designed to produce an eruption in six months. The members are praying and working toward the future ministry that each will move on to when the group officially ends. (This plan to end decisively and fruitfully is what constitutes the volcano clause.)

So far, as gifts have been identified and exercised, it seems that Michael and two other members will be trying to start a mission group working with youth. Joy is considering membership in an existing group which puts on lunches for students, and two of the study leaders who live only a few blocks apart will be launching a neighborhood Bible study. Sally and a couple of younger Christians in the group will collect a new set of people to begin another nurture group experience. Anticipation is mounting as everyone waits to see what God will do as a result of the investment each has made in the group.

Truth and Consequences

How does the myth of the eternal group, which was illustrated by John's group, develop?

The first culprit is bad teaching about group dynamics. A false expectation that the good things a group enjoys for the first two or three years can go on forever is often created in the minds of group members. Another possibility is that an understanding of the logic of growth is missing—namely, that people should actually change and become equipped for new ministry experiences. Or there may be an assumption that one kind of group can accomplish every kind of growth in every person.

Nurture groups are designed to grow people in studying and applying the Bible personally, opening up to one another, exploring new kinds of worship, and risking in mission. Above all, nurture groups are intended to release people in the gift of how they have been made by God. Teaching about such groups is lacking when no expectation for growth and gift development is planted in the members, and when the ultimate outcome flowing from growth is not understood. We must always be prepared to ask this hard question of our basic small group program: What is the point of so-called growth that does not lead to people being motivated into new spheres of gift-expression and leadership?

We will eventually become dissatisfied with a group when it is no longer stretching us, when all that could be accomplished in that group has been experienced or at least attempted. In my first few months of coordinating the groups at my church, I often had people come up to me and say, "If you ask me to get into one more group and self-disclose to one more person, I will scream!" As I began to consider wearing earplugs, I had to ask myself whether these people were tired of groups in general, or were simply fed up with a certain kind of basic nurture group. I knew that it was not just because of a bad group experience. I had seen over and over again that even the best nurture experience with an intimate group of friends eventually grows stale.

Finally, I concluded that the real issue is that people are not meant to stay in the same place forever. Disciples must intentionally move on to new types of group experiences. Why? Simply because the kind of risky mission and teamwork which will continue the process of discipleship in our lives will not occur in a basic nurture group. Basic groups are for growing in friendship, spiritual disciplines and gift-awareness; mission

groups are for expressing teamwork, prophetic encouragement and mature leadership. Jesus knew that there was a time for the twelve disciples
to be together in basic training (which, by the way, included short-term
mission experiences for them) and a time for them to be propelled into
full-blown mission.

Mature folk need to become pioneers in situations where the truth and
love of the gospel has not been known (like the apostle Paul did with
his traveling mission group), or builders in an already existing ministry
(like the seven original social workers did in Acts 6:1-6). Either way you
will be exercising mature leadership within a team that has agreed to work
together in risky outreach.

A Good Ending Requires a Good Beginning

Small group training should impart an understanding of the mechanisms
of growth, and it should do this with the whole group and not just with
leaders. The curriculum of this training would include the idea of a
specific contract to which the whole group agrees, and which forms the
basis for review and redirection every six to eight months.

Paradoxically, beginning well with a contract forms the basis of ending
well as a group. Like the TV show M*A*S*H, the best groups go off the
air when their ratings are still high. The volcano clause, a commitment
to move into new types of discipleship and, therefore, new types of
groups, is a particularly important part of the group's last contract. This
phase should arise naturally after two or three years together, that is, if
motivation toward mission is kept alive throughout the lifespan of the
group.

I suggest three years as the longest possible length for a small group,
but this depends on the group—and the culture. When dealing with
reserved Canadians, I find that it takes more time for efforts for self-
disclosure to actually pay off. Barriers to true friendship are high in our
individualistic culture, especially in cities.

In my experience as both a campus InterVarsity Christian Fellowship staffworker and a college teacher I have found that even though the student world is more conducive to sharing deeply and quickly, there are poor results from ending groups too soon. Yet I am told by my African students at Regent College that the barriers to relationship are not so high in their context (at least within the same rural tribe). Perhaps nurture groups in Kenya or Burkina Faso could be of shorter duration. On the other hand, basic groups might have to last even longer than three years in parts of the world where relationships form less easily than in North America.

If the goals of friendship and gift-disclosure have not been accomplished after two (or at most three) years in a nurture group then they probably never will, at least not in that group. After so much time, a group usually has settled into a bad pattern, where the natural inertia of being together, and laboring under an agenda of low expectations with a laissez-faire style of leadership, takes hold and preempts change. Comfort masquerades as friendship. The tireless work of a lone leader replaces the maturing of gifts. In fact, groups can carry on this way for a long time, never deepening in friendship or discipleship. Such groups need to apply this word from Hebrews, "Let us leave the elementary teachings about Christ and go on to maturity."

It is fair to wonder if any exceptions to the two- or three-year rule exist. Actually, there is only one rule in group work—"It all depends." In fact, at least two kinds of groups can maintain a healthy life over a longer period.

The first type is usually small and lasts for years. It is comprised of very close friends who have covenanted to meet infrequently (no more than once a month and no less than annually) to maintain a basis for accountability and a platform for response in the case of major personal crisis. Often the members of such long-term accountability groups are in the same life situation in terms of work and family. My wife and I have a group of friends that might be on the verge of forming this kind of network. I have heard of some long-term groups that have met for twenty years, but only annually—often gathering from all over the North American continent. The point of meeting infrequently is to preserve time for other ministry involvements. Time management keeps such groups healthy.

The other type of long-term group is the mission group which mature disciples form around a specific mission goal. In contrast with the accountability group, such groups usually meet every one or two weeks, and can in certain cases grow quite large over the years. An example of a mission group that can last for a long period is the drop-in Bible study for believers. Its mission is to act as a net for newcomers to the church until they are invited to be part of a regular nurture group. Forums for seekers would also fall into this category, where the leadership core acts as a mission group. As long as the agreed-upon goal of a mission group is being accomplished, it can continue and do well.

Going from Bad to Worthless

Undisciplined programming intensifies the problem of groups that do not know when to end. Take, for example, the case of appointed group leaders who have always wanted a flock to watch over (and dominate). This leads to one-person shows, lecture-style Bible study, and, in the worst cases, abuses of authority. Groups are coerced or seduced into continuing forever.

Churches can also perpetuate the myth of an eternal group by constantly feeding new members into a group or supplying co-leaders to support an existing leader who is bored, buried or burned out. Sometimes direct pleas or more subtle messages from the church leadership encourage a group to continue on for the good of the kingdom. The very absence of permission or lack of tradition about closing down a group speaks volumes to ears tuned to "commitment" and hearts turned to "service."

What the program ends up with is two types of unhealthy groups—

large and flabby or small and intense. The first type is often a drop-in Bible study built around a warm host or a wise teacher; a gregarious and articulate couple can keep such a group going for years and no doubt some good things would be happening at every point. However, a program based on this model alone would have many weaknesses—true intimacy would be missing in the midst of a sea of ever-changing faces, gift expression and leadership development would be difficult among the (usually) large membership of each group, and a joint mission project would have little chance of taking root.

A variation on the large and flabby theme is the group that has only become interested in socializing. This happens because the purpose of the group has been fulfilled, but the members have not yet admitted it. Consequently, they develop into a club more than a group. Members begin to say things like, "I'll drop in once a month, if I can."

Another rare possibility is that the large group develops into a church within a church, a collection of people with such strong bonds, mature worship (sometimes including the sacraments) and dynamic mission that they would keep going even if the sponsoring organization disappeared. In fact, frequently the members of this sort of group are drawn from a number of congregations, so the allegiance to any one congregation is weak. Although this development can be problematic in the eyes of some church leaders, I have heard that innovative congregations actually build their whole life around the house church model. If you are in a house church rather than a house group, the two- or three-year rule does not and should not apply.

Turning to the second outcome—the small and intense variety of group—one finds steadily decreasing benefits to the faithful members left behind. The same personal problems are worked on over and over again. This is what John's group experienced. Smallness comes about because dissatisfied members begin to dribble away; intensity arises because the remnant becomes more determined to make it work. New members are seldom welcomed into these groups. Actually, this might be a blessing; it is so difficult for any fresh input to compete against the emotional baggage and unwritten rules of the group that new volunteers often become victims.

Both of these negative group patterns—large and flabby,and small and intense—have one further detrimental effect on a groups program: they do not consciously and deliberately spawn new groups and new kinds of groups. However, the grassroots generation of groups is vital to a healthy program. Jesus came to make all things new, including the new wineskins represented by new groups.

After working this theory for three years in our local church, I began to see the fruit of new ministry and mission emerging from the basic group tree. This included a group seeking to reach out to a family housing complex and another interested in befriending people involved with recreational activities on the weekend. Both of these groups came to life because key people understood that basic nurture groups were not the only path to growth and discipleship.

To Do and Not to Do

Leaders of group programs should know how to plan for prevention and intervention when faced with the "forever" group mentality. To begin with, there are several bad responses:

1. Decree. Try to shut the group down. Groups become remarkably lively when they sense bureaucratic interference. There is no better way to turn a long-term group into an eternal one. If the hierarchy insists on stopping the group, it will simply go underground or disband into a collection of resentful individuals.

2. Dabble. Try to add new members or leaders (usually under pressure from the group). This is not a compassionate plan (from the point of view of the new member or leader, especially). Another unwise approach is to try to add a mission project. This at best adds another struggling year of life to the group.

3. Stall. Wait for signs of bad group patterns, such as flabbiness or intensity—and then move in with corrective teaching, or pray that the members will see the light.

4. Euthanasia. Ignore the problem group, cutting off all life support to hasten its death. This kind of group death is usually not a pretty sight.

5. Hope. Without taking any action, simply hope that a nurture group will transform into a mission group. This almost never happens.

Instead of using these ineffective approaches, you will find that, just as with the human body, the best kind of medicine is preventative:

1. Teach. Help entire groups understand the content of this chapter as they form.

2. Publish. Use periodic training notes as reminders. Reinforce the ideas in leader meetings.

3. Model. Point to alternative models that are working. Stress the excitement of branching off into new groups after two or three years.

4. Share. Give testimonies about contracts and volcano clauses that have worked. Create a climate of expectation.

The Last Rites

When you inherit unhealthy, long-term groups, or they develop in spite of your educational efforts, then you can only resort to a few (rather inadequate) steps of intervention. Begin by visiting the group and encouraging whatever good is resulting from their activities—especially anything that seems to be preparing members for future ministry. Take the leaders aside and make sure they know that there is permission for the group to end.

If members come to you and claim that their group should be ending—and you think they are right—tell them to leave cleanly, without a sermon to the other members. Groups are seldom responsive to advice from people they view as "traitors." What the departing members could do is ask the group to pray for them, specifically about a sense of gifting, leadership and vision in future group ministry. In this way, a good model would be laid out that may spark a good end for the whole group.

If you are invited to the group to troubleshoot, first listen carefully. Next ask a simple question: What do each of you want to get out of or contribute to a group? This will usually reveal the important issues. Pray for a creative way for them to end well. (A healthy end is easily recognizable: the people are willing to try a new group experience after little or no sabbatical time.) Make a couple suggestions. Gently and briefly share a summary of this chapter. Then leave them to make their own decision.

Finally, if a group is in its death throes and members are doing overt damage to one another, take strong leadership. Help both leader and members process feelings and celebrate the years of growth together. Your goal is to conserve people for a better group experience in the future. Try to have them focus on this next step in their discipleship process.

In general, do not ignore problem groups but do not spend all of your time with them either. Starting new, healthy groups like Sally's is the best way to help eliminate negative patterns in the long run.

All's Well That Ends Well

The world terminates things badly, with a thud. Jobs end with a pink slip, classes end with exams, marriages end with divorce. Christians need to set a better example. The leaders usually have to take some initiative in this, even if their role has been reduced during the mature phase of the group. Why? Because groups, even those who have planned to end in a disciplined way, will experience amnesia toward the end.

People say things like, "Let's not worry about a final meeting—we can still get together from time to time." Or "It's no big deal—we can still see each other at church." The problem is that sporadic contact and individual friendships are not the same as a sustained group life. The fact that a group experience is coming to an end simply must be faced square-ly, or there will be emotional baggage, unfinished business, and a sense of blockage for some when it comes to joining a new group. For example, if one member really believed that there would be frequent reunions, and therefore did not really say good-by to the group, then there could be a lot of resentment when the reunions do not happen (and they usually don't). Clean breaks are harder, but they are better.

Here are some steps for the leader and the group to consider when a group is in its terminal phase:

1. Begin praying six months before the end, focusing mainly on the possible visions for ministry which may be followed by individuals or subsets of people from the group.

2. Let members explore their sense of gifting in an exaggerated way. Study leaders can handle all of the studies; pastors can manage all of the community-building; worship leaders can experiment with new forms and so on. This can be a lot of fun, and a confirmation of the gifts people have.

3. Set an exact ending date.

4. All of the above should be put clearly in the final contract as part of the "volcano" clause.

5. As the final meeting approaches, plan a big party. There should be an opportunity to express joy and thanksgiving for everything that hap-pened in the life of the group. Commission one another into the new ministries that have been identified over the preceding months.

6. You may want to hold a "wake" before the party, giving a chance to have any feelings of regret, relief or resentment brought out in the open as the group draws to a close. If honesty is not possible by now, then it is just as well that the group is ending!

7. Avoid making unrealistic promises about reunions.

I have experienced both good and bad group endings. I have no doubt which I would go for, if I had the choice. Even if you think that your group is unhealthy, it is still good to end in the way just described. The "wake" may be more painful and the party more abbreviated, but it is still better than dribbling to a finish. Additionally, groups should consider going through some of these steps when any key member is leaving—in a real sense, the existing group will be coming to an end and a new one starting.

But It Seems So Calculated!
These guidelines are calculated—calculated for the kingdom. However, as with any hard analysis of social dynamics, there inevitably will be objections. Some might ask how we can suggest that people turn off the friendship tap after only two or three years. Surely stopping a group is not how good friends should act?

The answer is that we must distinguish between ending groups and ending friendships. The end of a group only marks the end of a particular kind of relationship structure. Naturally, you can be friends with whoever you want from the group for as long as you want, providing you are willing to make the extra effort required when a regular meeting no longer exists.

Four possibilities can be laid before a group to "soften the blow" of termination: they could plan a few reunions, a subset of the group could reform around a new mission, the new groups formed can maintain a loose or tight network, and real friendships can continue anyway.

I have experienced these alternatives personally. Two couples from a group that my wife and I belonged to several years ago are today among our closest friends, and another member of that group (who actually was a thorn in my flesh at the time) has become a close comrade since the group ended. Immediately after the same group shut down, Sharon and I went on with one of the couples to start an evangelistic study. Recently, the four couples that made up the original group played softball together. We are thinking about having a reunion party and catching up on the latest developments in our families (including four new children). Going even further back, to college days, I recall how my first roommate and I were in several different types of study, prayer and mission groups together (last week he and I counted six). Later, Mike was best man at my wedding, and this summer the nine members of our expanding families will share a cabin together at camp.

Good groups never die, they just become good friendships.

Ending is inevitable. The only thing you are trying to prevent is ending badly. End when things are still going well, when you are still friends. It is true that there is always pain attached to the voluntary ending of a group (even if the ending elicits a sense of relief rather than that of loss). But there is also a wonderful opportunity for God to make all things new—new wineskins for new life and new mission. Remember that even Jesus' group of apostles came to an end.

CHAPTER 2

• • • • •

MYTH #2

Groups should not be cliques

"Starting a home church is fine, but do you think we could pray a bit more about the location?"

I was thrilled, but also a little apprehensive. I had just gotten off the phone after talking with one of the young "bright lights" in the small group program I coordinate. He and his wife lead a group of about twelve folks. The group has been "gelling" nicely since it began six months ago. The ice has been broken, the members have become friends, and consequently there has been a high commitment to attending meetings. They have demonstrated an important principle: attendance problems never arise when a group is worth coming to.

So what is the problem? In fact, the leader is starting to feel agitated. He is worried about the group becoming too comfortable, not growing or being stretched. Also, he is convinced that growth requires a specific kind of stretching, that is, having non-Christians join, thereby turning the group into an outreach Bible study.

Both his concern and his plan are common ones, and they embrace part of the truth. First, this leader recognizes that it is bad when people get too comfortable in a group—when the group gets stuck in a set pattern of life together. So it is good that the leader wants to encourage this group to move on and go deeper. Second, the leader is right to identify outreach or mission as an essential component and catalyst of Christian growth. As Paul said to Philemon, "I pray that you may be active in sharing your faith, so that you will have a full understanding of every good thing we have in Christ" (v. 6).

Where then had this leader gone wrong? Quite simply, he had a jaundiced view of Christian cliques.

Open Says-a-Me

Open-door policies in a group can arise in four ways: (1) They are imposed by the leader. The leader tells the group that only one type of group is possible in his or her view, namely, one with an open membership approach. The group goes along because they are intimidated or inexperienced. (2) They are imposed by the program. The church organizers only permit an open-group style to develop. (3) They are imposed by default. Although not actually discussed in explicit terms, the assumption from the start is that the group will be open to new members, and this becomes the de facto policy once aggressive members start inviting new people. (4) They are "imposed" by the group. The whole group consciously agrees to the policy of inviting new members and the details get written into the contract.

The first three avenues to establishing an open door seem flawed in obvious ways. They rely, respectively, on bad views of leadership, bad operation of the church hierarchy, and bad group dynamics. In each case, the approach is incorporated in an undesirable contract. How has this come about? By the contracting process being abbreviated through an imposed or assumed ideal about group membership. At first sight, the fourth manner for establishing open groups seems better—a conscious and shared contract. This in fact may be so; as we will see below, there are types of groups which quite rightly should agree to an open membership policy. However, it is just as likely that even an explicit group agreement allowing new members has arisen in a bad way, leading to bad results.

When I first started to coordinate a local church group program, I quickly discovered that I had inherited a number of sad cases. There were folks who would come up to me sheepishly in the church lobby and say under their breath, "Do you think I could be in a group with the same people for a little while so that we can develop some real friendships?" Often these folks had been in a group with a conscious contract, but the open membership clause in that contract was wearing them down. Equally often, these people were quiet, sensitive, and unassuming—the last people to speak up in a contracting session. They were no match for the gregarious crowd-lovers, extroverts and evangelists who can so easily dominate a meeting where a group contract is set. Another possibility is that there was a general ignorance in the group of the implications of an open group format. Unfortunately, the following rule (which we will establish) is not well known: open membership is not good for every type of group, and open types of groups are not what every person needs.

There are different types of open membership policies. First, a group may decide to allow guests of members to drop in on a one-meeting basis. This is designed to help with awkward social situations like when relatives or close friends are visiting. How can these folks be left at home without embarrassment as one goes off to a group meeting? I sometimes call the guest policy in a contract an "in-law" clause. Yes, I have invited visiting relatives to a meeting that I was leading: I understand the family feelings involved only too well. However, I do not advise this policy. Groups that do allow such freedom should at least establish a protocol for the sake of courtesy: the leader of the affected meeting ought to be warned that guests will be present.

Second, a group may decide to allow a member to invite a friend to try out or join the group at any time, but only after some discussion about the wisdom of growing in numbers at any particular point. A variation on this policy of prior discussion is that potential new members must be privately "checked out" before joining. Preferably, this happens before they are even asked to join, and usually before they come to a meeting. The suitability of a new member is established either through the description a sponsoring member gives of their friend or through informal contact between the other members and the candidate.

Third, all need for discussion may be eliminated from the contract. Members can invite new people to come to a meeting (and presumably join the group) anytime—without warning. Finally, this same open-endedness can also include people showing up without specific invitation. The group's meeting time and place are regularly publicized so that, explicitly or implicitly, people are given freedom to show up. The existing members never know what new face might be at a meeting. I call this the "open season" approach.

In practice, any group does eventually reach a perceived ceiling in terms of numbers—often when the members are piled to the ceiling! So every group does become closed sooner or later. The only question is how the closure will be managed. Why is it bad when the closure only happens haphazardly—and only later rather than sooner?

Doorways to Doom

Groups exist for a purpose, that is, in order to accomplish something. If open membership helps and does not hinder in achieving the stated purpose, then so be it. However, open membership generally is not an asset in nurture groups. Recall that these basic groups exist for two main reasons: to build friendships (and thus establish a level of vulnerability and accountability to spur one another on in discipleship), and to draw out gifts (and thus inspire vision for mission).

Growing friendships and trying out gifts require one thing—trust. Trust in turn requires lots of time linked together with the same folks. If we accept this premise, then we can immediately see the danger of open membership or, to put it differently, closed membership that is delayed or that does not last long enough.

What does a new face in a meeting do to a group? At the very least, it stops the group from going forward. Usually very little will be shared of a personal nature at that particular meeting. This is because vulnerability depends on confidence in confidentiality and mutuality of ministry. In both respects, the existing group and the new person are at a disadvantage; they simply do not know one another very well yet. Other aspects of group life could also be affected. Bible study dynamics may be thrown off, mission projects left undiscussed, the intimacy of worship reduced. Of course, the casual, short-term visitor, for instance, an out-of-town guest brought along by a member, does the least damage. At most, an ineffectual meeting will result. Any group can survive this, unless it happens at every other meeting. However, I still discourage even this low-key form of openness on the grounds that one can find little value in it, and that it sets up a bad precedent for other forms of open attendance.

In fact, it is hard to think of a type of group where casual visitors would be an asset. It is true that some settings, such as house churches, can welcome one-timers with great freedom, but such unique structures usually do not classify as small groups anyway (they usually are too large).

On the other hand, a small group which is so intense that a guest would not stand in the way of deep sharing probably is the last place a casual (or even a more serious) visitor would want to be! In my experience, out-of-town guests are very understanding of the prior commitments of their host, and usually welcome a night to themselves. It is the rare guest who would be hurt if left behind, or who would insist on coming along (especially if he or she knew something about the intimacy of groups). If the guest is only in town for the meeting night, then the host should be excused from attending to spend time with the guest.

A more serious threat to group life is posed by new members showing up to join a group. All the negative impact of the casual visitor applies, except that it extends over more meetings. If new faces show up regularly, the group never makes much progress in its life. This arises because groups go through some well-known stages in their development.

The early stages of a group are sometimes called *exploration* and *transition*. Exploration describes the early meetings where members are getting to know one another and the leader is modelling vulnerability. Transition occurs when the group seems to achieve a deeper level of trust and intimacy. Anyone who has been around groups much can remember meetings where this deepening happens. Different things can spark transition, and the accompanying feelings can be painful, though the result is appreciated by the group.

What happens when new members join a group is that the group is catapulted back into the exploration phase, and some standard questions are asked. "Can we trust this new person?" "What will he or she contribute?" "Can I trust this new group? "Do I have a contribution to make?" Transition, when the questions are decisively answered, has to happen all over again. The group never makes much progress in the action stage, when members relate and work together with maximum impact, for they are constantly integrating new people. In short, a nurture group that expends all of its time and energy on engroupment does not grow good friendships.

Such groups suffer in other ways. The main kinds of gifts that they develop are those related to hospitality, welcoming and (depending on the newcomer) pastoring the needy. Other gifts, like those involved with Bible discussion leading, healing prayer, worship, mission, and spiritual direction, are underused. Needs, especially those of less aggressive members, become unexpressed in such fluid and awkward settings.

Often the group must learn to deal with crowd control early on, and then later contend with dwindling numbers as people get drained by large meetings and constant newcomers. Open membership and large membership often go hand in hand, and neither are conducive to consistent attendance.

Finally, most open-style groups are doomed to terminate in an unsatisfying way, with a feeling only of relief. No wonder I keep meeting people who are tired of open membership.

Cliques Are Okay

What is the alternative? Simply put, I would propose Christian cliques— small, exclusive groups. A group of people with a common purpose bands together. This purpose is mapped out in a series of meetings which are informal and open. People are free to come and go. If the purpose revolves around nurture, that is, friendship-building and gift discovery, then the members will probably see the wisdom of consistent attendance and closed membership.

In building such groups, it is important to discuss matters like attendance and membership policy—do not let a policy be imposed by default. An unwillingness to talk about such things can signal that someone is secretly trying to control the outcome. For example, people wanting a policy of loose attendance (that is, show up to meetings when you can) will try to avoid discussing the matter at all. They might suspect that a majority would hold a different view. It is better for everyone to declare their preference on membership and take their chances. Anyone who does not agree with the majority view on membership (or anything else) is free to leave during the precontracting stage. The remaining members can then finalize the contract, have their first official meeting, and begin exploration.

I have started several groups by the process just described, and counseled many new groups to follow such a pattern. Invariably people have told me that the result was much more satisfying than their past experiences. They end up with a membership policy with which the whole group is truly happy. Most importantly, the group's purpose has not been sabotaged. My own experience has been that closed groups do produce closeness, or at least allow close friendships and an understanding of gifts to develop if so desired.

Closed-minded about Closed Groups

Why do people complain about open membership and long for closed groups only in whispers? It is because the open versus closed debate is an old one in small group work, and many prejudices have developed. Some people, some of them friends and colleagues of mine, simply do not like the idea of exclusive groups. The mythology opposing Christian cliques is firmly entrenched.

The objections usually start with a concern for all the people not in a group yet. Surely closed groups look bad in the face of this need? But no one group, no matter how open and no matter how large its meeting space, can accommodate literally every person they come across who needs to be in a group. Managing a church's small group problem by weakening its groups is no solution at all.

The concern then narrows to non-Christians. How can groups remain closed in the view of the urgency of the gospel? An impassioned argument is made for the ideal that every group calling itself Christian must have open doors—specifically, open doors for unbelievers.

This is a hard argument to refute as it seems so spiritual. However, I dare to say, "No, not every group should be an evangelistic study." My reasons are threefold. First, people can always express their witness outside of group life. Second, some people need to be in other types of groups, ones that build spiritual friendships and accountability. Evangelistic studies are in fact mission groups, and not everyone is ready to be in such groups. A final flaw in the argument is the fact that outreach groups can themselves decide to be closed in membership when the members—including non-Christians—prefer it that way.

I just recently met a Youth for Christ worker from New Zealand who had built a whole ministry around closed evangelistic Bible studies. So the debate does not mean deciding for or against evangelism, but rather deciding what type of membership structure is appropriate for each type of group.

I can hear your next question: "What about people who positively want to be in an open group (whether with believers or unbelievers)? Are they not being excluded by your exclusive groups?" Yes, if the open format means so much to them. And no, because they can simply start or join an open group, perhaps one reaching out to newcomers in the church, or to seekers. Whatever they like. Allowing the possibility and even the necessity of closed groups in no way eliminates the possibility and even desirability of open groups. The local church in which I have been working has been weak in the area of open groups. I would like to see more such groups, as long as the members were joining with eyes wide open to the hard work of operating a mission group.

Finally, the supposed clinching argument I most often hear is that the Bible knows nothing about closed groups. I could answer that the Bible knows precious little about modern small group programs at all. Instead, I like to forestall the debate when I do small group workshops by innocently asking, "Do you think that Jesus would have ever started a closed group?" The light bulbs go on very quickly.

My opponents do not give up easily. "The twelve apostles might have seemed like a good idea to Jesus, but we are not Jesus, and it is just safer to have open groups. Closed groups can too easily become cliques." By "cliques" they mean too inward, too intimate and too intense. I say that this is all an expression of false guilt. It is true that closed groups appear to be not very outward-focused. It is also true that mission is vital to the health of every group. However, it is not true to automatically equate mission-mindedness with taking on new members. There are many ways to skin the missionary cat, as we will see later.

The concern about intimacy in a closed group usually betrays a discomfort with intimacy in general, or a misunderstanding about true friendship. Friendship implies exclusion: "I am your friend, but not his." We can only have a finite number of close friends. I find one of the most ironic things about working with small groups is the resistance to the concept of closeness in a group. Even group members themselves seem embarrassed about their own closeness.

Why should this be so?

Most people, on reflection, agree that friendship-building is the whole point of being in a nurture group. Why then avoid the closeness that comes from closed membership? Perhaps because we are not so sure about making true friends after all.

How to Avoid Becoming a Bad Clique

I have not yet addressed the issue of intensity in closed groups. This is because it is a sore point. I criticized intense groups myself in the previous chapter.

By "intense" one probably means an inwardness that does exclude every outward focus, or which even produces a hostile stance toward the rest of the world. Often there are unhealthy patterns of introspection and prolonged intercession that never seem to produce any change in members.

One of my most painful experiences as a young Christian was when my best friend got caught up in such a group. Cliques are not always okay, and it is important to know how to avoid the bad ones. There are five key strategies for avoiding such groups.

First, build mission-mindedness into your beginning contract and never let it disappear.

Second, learn how to say "no" to people who want to join in a way that will not discourage them. Refer to your contract, pointing out the membership clause. Explain the value of closed membership. Give them this chapter. Groups should always know where to refer interested parties that they cannot take in.

Third, make sure you progress in healthy ways from cycle to cycle, making a new contract requiring deeper and more comprehensive accountability each time. Do not get into a rut that will produce intensity rather than holy intimacy.

Fourth, if you are not too full, consider adding one or two new members at the point when the contract is open for discussion, that is, between cycles. Make sure you add only those people who agree with the emerging contract and seem compatible with logistics dictated by the rest of the group (for instance, the need to contribute financially for a common babysitter). Note that nurture groups should not add folks too late in the life of the group (say after one and a half years). It will not be a great experience for the new member (too much group history with which to integrate and not enough time left to do it), and it will be an unnecessary distraction for a group that should be planning its timely demise.

Finally, every group should remember that it is at best a temporary clique. Most groups, and certainly every nurture group, are meant to end. Within two or three years the resulting friendships no longer need the hot-house environment of a group for maintenance. So relax and enjoy it while it lasts.

CHAPTER 3

• • • • • •

MYTH #3

Bigger
is
better

Remember John's group from chapter one? It had five members left after meeting for eight years. Three of the people were founding members. At its peak this group had sixteen members.

When I say "peak" I am referring to membership size rather than quality of group life. Too often people equate or confuse quantity with quality when assessing the vitality of a group. This is what happened to John's group. This is why it went from a total of sixteen members to only five. In fact, during the course of eight years the group had contact with over thirty people who were more or less members.

Why did most of these people not stay? There could have been many reasons, many of them legitimate, but the primary cause was that the group became too large.

In the range of problems faced by group "doctors," the experience of the eternal group is followed closely in seriousness by that of the bulging group. Although this problem may seem close to the issue of closed and open groups discussed in the preceding chapter, it really represents another set of group decisions.

It is possible for a group to have closed membership, but to have closed the barn door after too many horses entered.

Small Is Beautiful

I have borrowed this heading from a famous book by E. F. Schumacher. What is true in his mind of alternative economics is also true in group work—appropriate size is key. Specifically, keeping small groups small is essential to keeping them vital. When only a few people band together, then a nurture contract has a chance of being fulfilled.

Why is this true? To put it in personal terms, we can become friends with a group of people if there are not too many of them. We have limited capacity for making friends. Also, people feel free to participate when the group is fairly small. Even extroverts can feel intimidated, not to mention those who are more cautious about opening up.

In a small group we won't feel like we are taking up someone else's time, or constantly find ourselves competing to get a word in edgewise. Additionally, we will have a chance to hear from everyone else in the group—most groups, if they had their way, would like to know everything about every member.

In a small-sized group individual gifts will be more visible when not hidden in a crowd of gifts. Another way of putting it is that we won't be lost in the crowd, for in a very real sense the gift we bring is ourselves.

In the end, Bible study, sharing and prayer will all be more satisfying experiences when the group is smaller. The only exception at this point might be singing. Personally, I like to be drowned out!

Mostly, though, it is good that we cannot hide in small groups. Accountability and discovery of God's leading in mission will both be harder to avoid when we are facing a few friends each week. There is a greater possibility for trying formal leadership positions. Additionally, we cannot avoid the other members. We are forced to grow in grace as we get to know others and encounter their unlovely sides. In a larger group, we can hang back and assume that someone else will do the loving. In a smaller group, because needs are being met, and because we are being stretched in confronting the needs of others, the meetings are exciting, and we want to be there. So we show up.

Take prayer for example. Some people may be new to informal praying in groups. They may be from a tradition that does not practice conversational prayer much. Or they may be new Christians for whom the thought of spontaneous praying out loud might either put them off or make them extremely nervous.

In the first case, objections to conversational prayer should be raised and alternatives proposed (using a prayer book, silent prayer) during the contracting phase—even before the group has officially begun. Reaching a compromise on such issues is usually easier with a smaller number of voices involved in the debate.

The smaller group is even more effective in the second case, however, when someone is simply afraid to pray aloud. Although there are several techniques (and books) that are useful at this point, nothing helps a person to get over the jitters more than practicing in front of a smaller group of people they know and trust.

Smallness is not only a powerful ally for group members, but also for leaders. As I have already indicated, this is true for someone chairing a contracting session, as well as for discussion, Bible study, sharing, prayer, mission planning, and certain forms of worship. Leaders love groups which are truly small. In fact, groups which are too large effectively eliminate many people from trying leadership.

Different gifting and experience are needed in different sizes of groups. As some growing churches discover only painfully and belatedly, people who could lead worship well when the congregation had fifty members are not appropriate in the pulpit when meetings top two hundred in attendance. The same thing applies when comparing groups of ten and twenty members.

Simple arithmetic explains why groups with more members have more complicated dynamics: when a group has n members the number of different interpersonal relationships involved are n times n minus 1 divided by 2 (trust me).

So a group with ten members comprises forty-five relationships, whereas a group with twenty members has 190 relationships affecting its group's dynamics. (The numbers are even higher if you factor in internal dialogs or communion with the Holy Spirit!)

One of my favorite teaching tools at small group seminars is an overhead transparency showing a cartoon figure of a leader surrounded by about twenty members. The leader is crying.

Big Is Usually Useless
In stating so baldly that big groups are bad, I need to qualify what I mean.

What I am referring to are groups that claim to be small but in fact are not. Of course, there are some legitimate big groups—Sunday services, social events, and youth group rallies. Various large and intermediate groups have their place in churches and organizations, as long as three things are kept in mind: such groups have different dynamics than small groups; such groups fulfill different purposes than small groups; and such groups cannot fulfill the purpose of small groups.

What happens in a group which is small in name only? For example, a nurture group with seventeen members, more or less. Saying "more or less" identifies the first problem—such bulging groups never seem too sure who their members are.

I always know I am dealing with a bad situation when a straightforward question like "How many members do you have?" produces vague answers. For instance, I might get a response like, "Well, we have about seventeen people on our list, no, nineteen, but only half that come to any one meeting."

Sometimes the answers are more creative, involving categories of membership: people who are in the core, people who come from time to time (especially to events involving food), people who drop in when they are back in town, or simply people the group continues to worry about even though they never turn up. Such "associate members" can be thought of as satellites that turn up regularly and relatively frequently or perhaps as comets who only blaze into the group every few months. Associate membership is rarely a positive experience for a group, although the impact depends on the type of group and the energy it takes to manage all of the hangers-on.

I know of one unique group which has been going for so many years that its annual reunion includes over fifty people. This group has a great time. But much more often a cloud of quasi-members is symptomatic of a group which is too large, and the burden of managing such a group is only made worse.

What are the other symptoms of swollen groups? The following are prevalent:

Now You See Them, Now You Don't. Attendance consistency in large groups is usually poor. This is simply because people's needs are not being met. Attendance is one of the most reliable signs of whether a group is doing its job. Ironically, one of the standard defenses I hear from too-large groups is that a reasonably small number of members turn up at any one meeting. The problem is that the faces at the meetings are always different, and this is hardly conducive to building trust and deepening relationships—not to mention the discouragement it produces in leaders.

For example, with a ten-member group, it is rare to have more than two people missing from any one meeting, that is, anything lower than eighty per cent attendance. On the other hand, in my experience it is not uncommon to have only twelve members from a twenty-member group show up—a drop to sixty per cent attendance. A much better way to have meetings of reasonable size and consistent attendance is to start with a membership of reasonable size.

Fatal Distraction. Most groups like to have members show up at meetings, even when they neglect to put a formal "attendance clause" in their contract (something like, "All members will attend each meeting except in the event of death, disaster or other act of God"). However, no matter how much a too-large group talks about attendance, it will inevitably be dissatisfied with the results. This sets up a feedback response of more talk (preferably constructive, but usually grumbling). Attendance can in fact become an obsession with large groups. The leaders spend an inordinate amount of energy getting everyone there. Occasionally, everyone does turn up at a meeting—usually when some good food is involved—and then the coordinator has a new problem: What do you do with so many people?

Slippery Slope. Members who value consistent attendance or smaller meetings to enable friendship-building eventually become fed up with "disenchanted evenings" and can—after sporadic attendance—drop out altogether. This causes a strain on the leadership and a further drain of energy as the group worries about the missing member.

After peaking in membership, like John's group did for a few weeks, there will be a gradual decline in numbers. The slide is usually not reversible because group tiredness and discouragement has set in too deeply. Such groups often develop into tiny, faithful bands that can struggle on for years, bitterly pining for the glory days when the meeting room was full.

Disappointing Liaisons. Poll the members in a group which is too large and you will find many that are secretly unhappy. The reason is simple: the promise that brought the group together in the first place, the goal of making friends and growing in grace, is subtly sabotaged when meetings are overfull. When a structure defeats the best intentions of those involved, it is the greatest and most ironic tragedy of all.

The Other Side
What may seem self-evident in the name "small group" is missed by many who allow groups to become too big to be classified as "small." Others actively pursue large and growing memberships. Their motivations are manifold.

First, some people seem unable to distinguish size from success. This is not surprising given the culture in which we live, a culture which has thoroughly infected churches and other Christian organizations. However, we must resist the myth that big is better.

I am constantly meeting group leaders who are embarrassed because they do not have larger groups, as if numerical growth alone guaranteed quality. Just like the rule which finds nurture groups lasting a year too long, there seems to be another rule which would have groups add six more members than they need. This ambition in fact leads to their downfall.

Other leaders see enlarging their groups as a virtue because it ensures good numbers at meetings—out of twenty members, twelve are bound to show up. They never seem to ask the question, "What is wrong with small meetings, anyway?" In fact, they will get to answer this question themselves in the end because, as we have seen, that is exactly the kind of meeting that large groups will generate. So why not start with smaller meetings to begin with, and avoid getting there the hard way?

Sometimes people are very aware of the kind of dynamic set up by large groups in small-group clothing, that is, inconsistent attendance and a certain amount of anonymity. Secretly, this dynamic suits them because they are afraid of the intimacy of a true small group. A purported distaste for cliques often masks a fear of growing close to people. It is too bad that the fall-out from large groups—tiny, discouraged groups—falls into the very trap that large memberships are supposed to avoid.

Some people boldly insist that larger groups do a better job of group activities. Usually they are referring to singing. They have me there. Singing can be pretty terrible in a group of seven or eight folks (especially if I am one of them). And it is true that there are more musical gifts and instruments available, on average, in a larger group.

I have two replies. First, the nuisance of weak singing is not enough reason to form a large choir and abandon the fruit of friendship and freedom which grows in the smaller group. Second, who says that a group has to sing, anyway?

But surely, you might ask, in every activity—Bible study, prayer, sharing—there will be more energy in a larger group? This is only true for those leaders and members that thrive on a larger stage. Quieter people suffer in the larger group where two or three members dominate by talent and charisma—or volume. In fact, the larger the group, the more structured the leadership must be. Increasingly, people's gifts become less used. The group's agenda and life are less democratic. This is as good a place as any for a small confession. I have been unfair, or at least incomplete, in describing the fate of the larger group. Some of these groups, rather than shrinking, actually maintain a goodly size for months or years. The bad part is that the membership only appears stable. In reality there is a constant turnover of members.

What holds this kind of group together? Usually it is one or two strong leaders who are exercising a shepherding role over the group. These leaders have some characteristic which is attractive to others for a time, such as a pastoral nature or Bible-teaching skill. New Christians in particular can be captured by the wise guidance (at best) or dogmatism (at worst) originating with an elder in the faith. However, as they mature, people eventually become disinterested in the strictures of these groups. They would like to lead a study or share an opinion sometime! Nevertheless, even as disgruntled people move on, the leader is very effective at finding new recruits for his or her flock. The group is maintained at a size that keeps the leader happy.

Now this kind of group may even have a place in a church or other organization, especially if it fits in with an overall strategy of groups. The real danger comes when the flock leader is a complete maverick rather than a "benign dictator" in sympathy with the elders of the organization. Or when the elders confuse this kind of group with true small groups where there is a mutuality of ministry and leadership.

Program planners can fall into a very common trap which leads to unhealthy membership sizes—the idea of multiplying groups by expanding and splitting existing groups. There are three main reasons this does not work.

First, we have already seen that groups rarely get to a size of, say, twenty with any kind of healthy life or consistent attendance. It is hard to imagine such a group ever reaching the maturity to have a general meeting where all members agree to divide neatly into two groups of ten. Second, whatever its size, a group usually does not see the logic of dividing into two halves which will do roughly what the group now does together. The virtue of numerical growth in the group program is rarely compelling enough to disturb friendships. Indeed, groups will find virtually any excuse to avoid being "split." More subtly, even if a group is coming to the end of its life, it usually is precisely because a majority of members do not want to be in a nurture group anymore. The last thing they want to do is start two new groups of this same type. Finally, I must report that after consulting with dozens of group programs over the years, I have never seen the "grow and split" strategy actually be effective to any extent.

My Number Is Up

You may have noticed an odd fact. I have been talking for several pages about groups which are too large but have never defined what "too large" represents. Indeed, I have been throwing some numbers around in examples, but have not said where those numbers come from. It is time for me to come clean and answer the question which is (I hope) on every reader's mind by this point: What is the perfect number of members for a small group?

Roberta Hestenes suggests 3-12 members in her definition of a small group. Three is the lower limit because two people are not a group. They can only have a conversation. Contrary to what some think, the magic number twelve for the upper limit does not come from the number of apostles Jesus chose. Instead, it is a rough guideline that correlates with other natural limits imposed on a group. These limitations fall into the categories of meeting purpose, meeting space, and meeting time.

First, different purposes allow for different sizes. Mission groups can be larger than basic nurture groups, which in turn can be larger than deep accountability groups. The size has mainly to do with expectations held by members as to the extent of personal reflecting in each meeting. While all types of groups should include sharing and prayer, some groups, like accountability groups, invest more here than other groups.

Another factor affected by purpose is the logistics of getting together.

For example, mission groups often meet less frequently (and for a longer period) than nurture groups and therefore can accommodate a larger number of busy people. On the other hand, accountability groups that have decided to meet long-term over many years usually need small memberships because of the complexity of coordinating diverse schedules and locations for rare meetings.

Additionally, one could conceive of a group built around some kind of exercise or activity that would in turn shape the membership size. For example, certain spiritual disciplines come to mind. A strict program of prayer partnerships would obviously require an even number of members. Alternatively, some mission tasks require a minimum number of people and gifts, and the group dynamics simply must be modified to work with that number of people.

A second limitation on group size is the dimensions and layout of the meeting space. This may seem obvious, but I have often seen the key principles about space ignored. People should be comfortable, not wedged into a hot, claustrophobic space. Any group can handle one or two meetings with poor square footage available, but eventually smelly armpits and small armchairs can slay a group.

As Roberta Hestenes puts it, groups are to meet "face to face." This is to be taken literally. Everyone should be able to see everyone else.

I was once in a very full meeting where a couple of people had to sit on the floor. They contributed nothing all evening as they were never brought into the conversation through eye contact with the leaders. In addition, people should never sit in multiple rows or, if possible, in a straight line (you don't want three or more on a couch). The ideal, of course, is to meet with members in similar seating in an approximate circle. The number in the group may have to be tailored according to the available space.

The third limiting factor on appropriate membership is the typical meeting length which is agreed on. This limitation is perhaps the most fundamental and yet also the most neglected. The key assumption here is that everyone should make a contribution each meeting that suits the purpose of the group. Naturally, this takes time, and more time is required when there are more members.

Assuming that we are dealing with a nurture group with adequate meeting space, a good rule of thumb is to allow about 10-15 minutes on average per member. Roberta Hestenes, with an upper limit of twelve in her definition, might be assuming a regular meeting duration of more than two hours, or a certain number of absentees each time. I am not sure that either assumption is valid, so this number may not be a good upper limit for typical small groups. Remember there will usually be at least one person with a crisis at each meeting. That person will take up more airtime than 15 minutes.

How does the formula work? Take the amount of time the group is able to meet and divide by 15 minutes. For example, many downtown and campus ministries operate lunchtime groups that have at most sixty minutes. Sixty divided by 15 would suggest that 4 members would be an optimal number for the group. (Probably 3 would be better, given the time spent in traveling). Following this rule will ensure that the group members will actually feel "heard" in the meeting.

Such an analysis would revolutionize many organizations built on brief nurture meetings. Consider what should happen to class sizes in the adult Sunday-school "hour"!

Generally, church and residential campus small groups plan to meet for one and one-half to two hours in an evening, for example, from 7:30 to 9:30 p.m. Therefore, they often can accommodate 8 to 12 members comfortably (based on a more conservative formula of ten minutes per member). On the other hand, house churches that meet for four or five hours each week can easily grow to 20 or more members.

Given this, you can see why overly large groups report that their meetings go on far too long. Even one or two members beyond the natural limit can cause a meeting to drag on in spite of good intentions to end on time. Groups that are too large face a difficult choice—midnight meetings or unheard members. After bad contracting and broken confidentiality, uncontrolled meeting time is probably the most common reason for people being turned off from a group.

So far we have been talking about the upper limit in small groups. However, a group may definitely opt to have a smaller group than its absolute maximum. Why might a group do this? Simply to provide each member even more time to talk, to not talk, to pray, and so on.

My wife and I have been in more than one group that could have taken ten members but voluntarily limited itself to eight. There is a wise lower limit as well. Having only three or four members in a two-hour meeting is possible but not usually advisable. The temptation to coziness or intensity is too great. For example, I hesitate to call two couples (especially if they were already friends) getting together regularly a true small group.

Additionally, a group could start out smaller than its ultimate goal with a view to adding one or two members at a re-contracting point later. This is a temporary limit. However, I need to point out two cautions for those taking this approach. Do not try to add either too late or too many. Both styles of growth are awkward as groups quickly become set in their ways. For example, a group should probably not start with only four members with a plan to add four more in a few months. To attempt this can easily lead to competing contracts where the relatively large number of newcomers do not want to adopt the established life of the founding four. It would be better to find only one or two people to fit in. To put it another way, the starting size of any group should be pretty close to its final size.

How to Lose the Battle of the Bulge
There are many pressures that can force a group to become too large. These pressures come from leaders who feel insecure about small (and, they suppose, unsuccessful) efforts. They can come from members who

feel sympathy for all the ungrouped in the world and friends of members who desperately want in. Or they can come from group planners who are panicking in the face of so many pastoral and discipling needs in their organization, combined with a lack of knowledge about how to build a group program effectively.

Complaints can be vigorously thrown at groups which have reached their target size. Jim started the first group his church had known six months ago. It has a full complement of members. Many leaders in the church were wondering why the group could not expand. So far the group has held firm to its ideal size, knowing that this will be best for the church in the long run. Recently, I found out that some key support for the resolve of Jim and the other members had come from the pastor of the church. This is very encouraging.

Organizers of group programs can be allies in the cause of good group size or they can be passive or active enemies. The passive oppression happens when they do not act as release valves, providing an opening for all appropriate candidates who want to be in a group, or as circuit break-ers, not allowing general inquiries from prospective members to get through to groups. In our church, we do not publish the names and phone numbers of group coordinators. They do not need the temptation or the hassle of phone calls from folks lobbying to get in. It is even worse for newer, lively groups. Their reputation as the hottest thing around brings many overtures from prospective members.

Usually the individual group is its own worst enemy as it has not learned the disciplines of "dieting"—watching for the warning signs of attitudes that lead to largeness, successfully resisting the temptation of candidates who want to swell the numbers, and knowing when to add and when to abstain. I have summarized a weight-watcher's checklist in Re-source Two. I recently encountered a textbook case—at least according to my textbook—which demonstrated the relationship between size, tim-ing and group discipline. The group had started with a very clear contract, and added a new couple (who matched the profile) at an appropriate point after one year. They fit in marvelously. However, another couple, equally qualified, had a very difficult time joining just six months later. Too much group life had passed under the bridge by that point. This year, two more couples wanted to join. The group wisely said no, and suggested alternatives. In fact, there was room in the group—some members had left—but the age of the group prevented the smooth incorporation of new folk. So size does not tell the whole story—timing is also an issue.

In my experience, people are generally respectful of a group's firmly held position on closed membership and optimum size and even grateful that they have encountered a group program that promises to be healthy because of its discipline. Naturally, there are some risks of offending when you are decisive about closing doors and limiting size. However, I believe that the risks are worth it.

There is nothing like a true small group where friendships are grown, where salvation is worked out in confession and accountability, where the three or eight are gathered in his name, where multiple hearts are taught by the Spirit, where gifts are explored in an atmosphere of trust, and where people are exhorted to be fools for Christ. We must be small in our groups and big in our dreams.

CHAPTER 4

• • • • •

MYTH #4

Groups
need strong
leaders

*"I like to think of myself as the facilitator and
enabler of this church rather than the senior pastor
or chief executive officer."*

met one of my group leaders over lunch. She is very promising—dedicated, thorough, pastoral. However, her leadership style could also become very problematic. I knew we were on dangerous ground when she began to tell me about plans to turn her relatively new group into an evangelistic Bible study. She said she knew this would stretch the members in just the way they need.

Not only do I have a problem with the plan, but I have a funny feeling about the process too. I quietly asked her, "What does the group think about this?"

Her reply was, "Oh, I know my members; I know they will have no problem with this idea."

I suggested that she ask them anyway, but I am not too hopeful that she will do it. For her, I think, the results would be too unpredictable.

Walking a Thin Line

This episode illustrates the thin line that exists between authoritative leadership and authoritarian leadership. The group suffers when the leader's hand is too heavy. Parenting can too easily turn into patriarchalism or patronization. And group initiative will be smothered.

Problems also arise when the expectations laid on the leader by the group are unrealistic. The leader is sometimes expected to have every gift, to do all the necessary tasks, and to play all the significant roles. The leader suffers when the load is too heavy. Of course, this message of total responsibility and competence is never spoken directly, but instead subtly with statements like "As you lead this group, you are the frontline pastoral worker of the church." The leader tries to rise to the occasion, then plunges to the earth with melted wings.

Whether a problem of domineering style or one of overblown expectation, the result is the same for the group: bad news. The only difference is that in the first case the leader persists in the delusion of knowing everything, whereas in the second case the leader permits the illusion that they can do everything. (Consult Resource Three for a checklist of danger signals concerning leadership style.)

Sometimes the signs of trouble can be program-wide. For example, there might be many tired leaders, veterans who do not want to lead, or mavericks who are not submissive to the overseers in the organization. One sign that is not so obvious is when a church has multiple leaders in most groups (for instance, placing two leadership couples in each group). I knew one church where three couples could be found as a leadership team in some groups. Imagine a platoon with six lieutenants!

Usually the push for multiple leaders comes from the leaders themselves, and usually it is because the job description assigned or assumed is too much for one person or one couple. I am not against leadership teams in general, but it is overkill within one small group. A dichotomy between leaders and members is too easily established—that is, if there are any members left over who are not classified as leaders! Not only is the result top-heavy and cumbersome, but too many potential leaders become concentrated in one group. This makes recruiting leaders to expand a program all the more difficult.

Mismanaging the Flock

Ezekiel 34 provides a clue to both types of group leadership problems, the overly oppressive and the overly paternal. First we read, "Woe to the shepherds of Israel who only take care of themselves! Should not shepherds take care of the flock? You eat the curds, clothe yourselves with the wool and slaughter the choice animals, but you do not take care of the flock. . . . You have ruled them harshly and brutally" (vv. 2-4).

This is an extreme description of the problem of oppressiveness. No group would stand for such an obvious fleecing of the flock. However, we do find groups putting up with leaders who are essentially sheep in wolf's clothing.

The fundamental flaw in such leaders is their self-centeredness. They feel that they know what is best for the group and (sometimes) for each member in the group. So they impose an agenda. Contrary to Ezekiel, the imposition is not often harsh and brutal, but instead quiet and subtle.

The leader creates a climate from the start that promotes his or her preeminence. The group may always meet at the leader's house. The leader might always sit in the "speaker's seat," usually a big, comfortable chair with a commanding view. I have visited groups where there is one particular chair used by the study leader. Out of deference, the members try to get me to sit in this seat.

Whether from one seat or many, the leader may guide—or, more frequently, teach—the Bible study for the first several meetings. The difficulty is that, as with other group dynamics, such study patterns are soon set in stone.

Another mechanism used by controlling leaders is simply to avoid any true contracting session, along with its built-in democracy. Contracting a group agreement is not a natural process for a group (especially in new groups) and therefore it requires initiative from the leader. If the leader does not take the initiative to facilitate a contract, it is easy for a group to fall into the habit of taking the leader's direction for everything instead.

Finally, a false culture of unity can be cultivated. The group is taught to value unity at all costs, and then disunity is defined as any diversity of opinion or gift. Under this culture, the group will tolerate any excess on the part of the leader, including the exclusion of members who dare to disagree.

What of the second group leadership problem—paternalism?

Returning to Ezekiel 34, we read: "You have not strengthened the weak or healed the sick or bound up the injured. You have not brought back the strays or searched for the lost" (v. 4). In other words, "you have not been truly interested in the group."

The problem of paternalism comes in through a correction of this attitude taken to an extreme. Sometimes leaders are so motivated to work for a group that they do all the work—every weak, sick, injured or lost member is their exclusive concern. The motivation for such overloaded expectations comes from the leaders themselves, from the group, or from the organization the group belongs to.

This leadership problem consists of too much responsibility, trying to reverse the errors described in Ezekiel 34 single-handedly. What is forgotten is that leaders are not created to do all things for all people. One human being does not possess all the gifts, energy and time to do everything needed by a group.

Breaking the Mold

Where do the various types of group leaders come from? The simple fact is that all leaders are not created equal. This is because people do not have the same personality or gifts in the beginning, and these traits are not reinforced through the same experience of leadership in life.

One way to understand the range of leadership types is to think of a spectrum with high dominance at one end and low at the other. Neither end of the spectrum is good for groups. We have been talking mainly about the dominating type, but the opposite extreme is just as bad: a "leader" who does not lead at all.

I seem to be encountering more and more leaders and groups which are proud of the fact that they have no real leader. These groups, especially new ones, with laissez-faire leadership suffer from the indecision that comes from too much democracy. An example once again is the process of contracting. We have already noted that the process can be actively thwarted by an insecure leader seeking to maintain control—but the same thing can happen with a passive leader who by nature takes no initiative. It is rare for a group to contract well without guidance.

Domineering leadership and undemonstrative leadership are both bad. However, these styles arise out of an individual's personality or gifting, rather than out of some malicious intent. The good news is that every leadership style can be somewhat modified through training.

I have one friend who has learned to chair meetings well in spite of the fact that he has a dominating style. He has moderated his aggressive tendency, wisely avoiding the common misconception that committees need driving leadership. Instead, he has learned that committees are relational arenas where people are given permission and support to do things. The success of my friend in (for him) a foreign environment is rare.

There is a place for every leadership style, even self-absorbed types, somewhere in an organization. The important thing is simply to avoid either extreme of the leadership spectrum when it comes to small groups. So who should lead groups?

Some might leave the preceding pages with the notion that I do not believe in leadership, or that I think leaders in groups should best know nothing or do nothing. "Nothing" could not be further from the truth. What is needed in the case of groups is the middle of the spectrum: leaders who are enough concerned for the group to forget themselves and to avoid the tendency to dominate or to do nothing.

The most helpful group leaders find themselves in the middle of the spectrum because of personality and gift, just like every other type of leader. Some lean a bit toward the dominating end of the spectrum. These are the "tellers," leaders with firm ideas who are not entirely closed to group input. They are different than the "commanders" at the extreme end, just as being authoritative is different than being authoritarian. Other middle-of-the-road leaders lean more toward the do-nothing end of the spectrum. These are the "sellers," who seek to have every member own each decision and activity. Clearly, though, this style is more active than that expressed by the "sleepers" at the extreme of this side of the spectrum.

Small groups generally need tellers or sellers precisely because their interest in the needs of the group is both genuine (unlike commanders) and active (unlike sleepers). Groups need to reinforce the kind of leadership which serves them best at the time. In fact, what happens with group leadership actually depends mostly on the group itself.

Corporate Codependency

In some ways groups get the leaders they deserve. There has been much popular literature lately about codependency, or the tendency for mutually destructive behaviors to attract one another. For example, those suffering from over-responsibility for the lives of others often end up enabling addictive behavior like alcoholism. Or chronic victims end up with abusive marriage partners or with teen-agers who persecute them. Likewise, whole groups can attract or enable authoritarian leaders or workaholic leaders in their midst.

Group members who are not inclined to make decisions or take initiatives end up with leaders who will do these things for them. The result is very bad for the group, and does nothing for the leader either. The behaviors are reinforced. The group becomes less capable of owning the direction or the work of the group, and it grows ever more dependent on the leader, who in turn rises to the occasion.

The real tragedy in this process is that the very purposes of the group become subverted. When decisions are made by the leader alone, members are not forced to love one another in grace. Disagreements produce growth; coming to consensus is the crucible of true friendship-building. On the other hand, when the leader does everything, the gifts of other members are not exercised and appreciated. Like muscles, these gifts can atrophy.

In short, the limits of freedom are not tested in the realm of personal expression and vision. So individual members suffer because they are not loved enough nor do they have enough opportunity to love. And because the true measure of a group's health is its weakest member, in the end the whole group suffers.

A Leader for All Seasons

In some ways I have been too hard on the overbearing and the over-worked, suggesting that both originate partly in personality flaws. From a psychological point of view, the truth is that all leaders, whether per-ceived as good or bad for small groups, will behave precisely in that manner that will make them feel successful. What is required is a new definition of successful small group leadership so that leaders of all stripes can have a sense of freedom to try a new approach.

We do not need strong leaders so much as sensible, sensitive and servant leaders.

Sensible leaders set the tone (regarding their limited knowledge and the necessity of their limited duties) from the start of the group. On no account should leaders ever come across as an exclusive expert on group dynamics, even if they have been to a seminar or read this book! Some-times a group will try to assign this status to a leader.

I remember being in on the launch of a new group which included a colleague who knew my background well. To my horror, this is how he introduced me at a pre-contracting session: "Dan is an expert, so we should let him set the agenda for our group."

What was my first act at our first meeting? I innocently asked, "How did you feel about my suggested role in this group?" Every member, even my friend, said with some emotion that they regretted how I had been introduced. They wanted the group to be truly their group, they wanted to play a part in shaping its direction.

Groups and leaders should avoid the rut of having the leader do all the leading. Here the solution requires more than rotating the Bible study leadership. Although sharing the study can be a useful start, the leader must also avoid other routines such as doing all of the praying, worship-leading, phoning, greeting and hosting.

Leaders should encourage all volunteers enthusiastically, and if they are not confident that voluntary involvement will happen, then they should recruit people to do real jobs from the very first meeting. Hospitality tasks like serving hot beverages and hanging coats are a good place to start. Members who are known to the leader can be asked to close in prayer or play the guitar. The pattern of solo leadership must be disrupted from the beginning, otherwise the group could get the wrong message.

In my first summer as a Christian, my roommate and I started two groups. On Tuesday evenings, I would lead the study, and he played host. On Saturday mornings, the roles were reversed. We were trying to model shared leadership.

Finally, in addition to limiting expectations about their expertise and their expenditure of energy, leaders should positively declare what they can contribute to a group. In other words, they should set out a reasonable and useful job description alongside any humility and honesty about their abilities.

Sensitive leaders are firm but flexible. First, they are aware of their particular leadership gifts and the style or personality in which they are expressed. They know that there are built-in limitations to how they lead, and they realize that such limits can only be moderated up to a point. There are several means of moderation for a leader:

☐ be real members in the group, always talking about "our group," never taking on the airs of a higher echelon of existence—be a leader in sheep's clothing

☐ be open to an "iron sharpening iron" experience, where members smooth the rough edges of your personality

☐ if you suspect that you are a bit authoritarian or too relaxed, then confess this to the group and ask them to pray for you and help you practice a different style

☐ be schizophrenic, behaving as a member but also as a "fly on the wall," observing the group process and watching out for complementary leadership gifts

☐ do not be threatened when members do begin to exercise leadership, recognizing that authority and responsibility must be shared

☐ be honest when you are frustrated or weary.

Leaders need to be direct about the gift they can contribute most and ask for an opportunity to share this gift. For example, I am a student of the Bible and would be discouraged if not given a chance to exercise this love in a group. Furthermore, a leader should be given lots of room to do the general coordinating tasks that the group says they want done. I have personally experienced the frustration of encountering resistance to the very leadership role I have apparently been assigned. If this happens, be sure to talk to the group about it.

Lastly, a leader must try to be flexible. Although it is a tall order, the ideal leader for a small group starts out as a "teller," taking lots of initiative in the contracting process and the exploration stage, and then becomes more of a "seller" as the group matures, allowing democracy, group ownership, and every-member leadership to flourish. This shift can be difficult for some leaders. If it proves impossible, the best thing is to let someone else become the leader. Later on, the "teller" may need to re-emerge to take a lead during termination—when members often miss the importance of ending well.

Servant leaders have a list of attitudes and skills that they bring as a worker to a group. I have good news and more good news about this. First, the list is not infinite in length. Second, the attitudes and skills can be learned. In Resource Four, I have provided an outline of the "overalls" of the worker, or seven spiritual disciplines, and the "toolbox" of the worker, or seven practical disciplines. There are many books that can give more details about this job description. *Good Things Come in Small Groups* would be a good place to start. One of the best ideas in that book is that leaders lead by serving and serve by leading. I say "Amen." The leadership role in a group is not discovered on a pedestal, it is found in the trenches.

What's in a Name?

A group and its leader can have great intentions, but the best leadership philosophy can be eroded by support mechanisms that may be missing in the group program of an organization. Ironically, the most valuable structural change might be to eliminate the word *leader* altogether as a label for the serving role just described above. Good alternatives are words like *facilitator, administrator* or, my favorite, *coordinator*.

The closest New Testament picture of this position might be in 1 Corinthians 12:28 where we find mention of a "helmsmen" or "those with the gifts of administration." Some Latin American communities use the term *animator*. The advantage of a name change would be to break tradition with what "small group leader" has meant in some circles, that is, a comprehensive, jack-of-all-trades position, and to focus on the more narrow (but still important) job description we have been advocating in this chapter. Furthermore, leadership could then be seen more broadly as something emerging from every member.

Next, the specific definition or job description of the coordinator needs to be clearly spelled out. Sometimes the exact opposite is done. Consider the title for a course sponsored by a theological school in our town, "Teaching Tips for Group Study Leaders." "Teaching" is usually not the best approach to group study.

The recruiting of coordinators needs to be reformed. First, the idea of linking coordinating to any particular gift needs to be removed. Group coordinators do not need to have the gift of pastoring nor the gift of study-leading. This may seem like heresy to some but doubters should simply review the job description in Resource Four. People with virtually any gift can learn these skills once the foundation of a servant heart is in place. Second, this relaxing of prerequisites means that coordinators can be drawn from a much wider pool of candidates. Recruiting is made easier. Third, recruiting and appointing can in fact be eliminated in some cases where coordinators are allowed to emerge from a group naturally.

It is best to stress on-the-job training, though formal contexts like seminars and courses can be a useful way to give people enough confidence to try coordinating a group and then later to interpret their experiences. The advantage of in-service training, aside from the common knowledge that learning by doing is the only true learning, is that it involves all the members in the process and helps to promote humility in leaders. An even better way to think about training is to focus on whole groups. Every member needs to be an informed ally supporting the coordinator in what they should and should not be doing. I would rather have a trained group and a novice coordinator than the reverse situation.

The Most Excellent Way
None of what I have been saying is intended to denigrate group leadership. By defining a precise coordinating job I hope to bring greater satisfaction and success to people in such roles, and thereby even greater honor than the false glory of power trips or busyness. The coordinator's job is as demanding as it is critical to the health of a group. However, being clear about coordinators also clears the way for something even more vital—the notion that the best kind of group leadership is leadership by the whole group. We need strong groups even more than we need strong leaders.

CHAPTER 5

• • • • •

MYTH #5

More members
should
lead

*I've asked Peter to give each of you a copy of this
week's discussion questions.*

I have to confess that I am cheating with the title of this chapter. The idea that more members in a group should lead is not exactly a myth. In fact, I actually endorse the idea.

So why do I label as a myth the notion that "more members should lead"? Simply because it usually means the wrong thing in people's minds. Or, if not, the sentiment still does not go far enough. And, as we will see at the end, a subtle shift in viewpoint allows an even healthier way of looking at group leadership. We begin by demolishing a myth within a myth.

Bodies Are Not All Mouth

In the famous passage of 1 Corinthians 12, Paul writes: "Now the body is not made up of one part but of many. . . . If the whole body were an eye, where would the sense of hearing be? If the whole body were an ear, where would the sense of smell be?" It is sad how often small groups in churches and other organizations seem to forget this principle. How? Quite often by trying to turn everyone into a "mouth"—that is, by having every member regularly take a turn leading the Bible study. Nine times out of ten, when a group talks about shared leadership it is referring to this policy of rotating the study preparation and presentation.

I have visited many groups in which painful studies have resulted from just such a policy. The selected study leader has been ineffective, and so the study has been directionless, chaotic, boring or interminable. To allow this to happen to the Bible is criminal, especially in an age when people are already a little jaundiced concerning the relevance of the Scriptures. How does this unhelpful view of shared leadership arise in a group?

First, the group may not have contracted consciously (or thoughtfully) around the issue of rotating the Bible study leadership. Or it has just assumed that no other model of study leadership is legitimate.

Second, the group may adopt the common legend that says every believer should be able to lead folks effectively in a Bible study. Although I do believe that almost anyone can be trained to act as group coordinator, some people will never be able to lead studies well. To believe otherwise is the same as saying everyone has the gift of pastoring or evangelizing. In fact, leading good Bible discussions requires a subtle mix of skills and gifts. To insist that everyone should be able to do it is cruel and unusual punishment for members and groups alike.

Third, the rotation of the study is often handled unwisely. A typical style involves passing the study guide on to the next person in line, with little or no advice from an experienced study leader. The novice then descends into the pits of despair for a week while sweating out the preparation and having anxiety attacks about the coming meeting. Not only is active encouragement during this process limited, but evaluation following a study is even rarer. Groups seldom risk giving the kind of feedback which might actually produce a good study leader one day.

Fourth, unwilling volunteers fall back into unhealthy study patterns. They commonly overprepare, spending too many hours in secondary sources. How many of us have blanched as we watched a study leader enter the meeting weighed down by commentaries? Alternatively, leaders lacking confidence can follow a published study guide too slavishly, producing a stilted and straightjacketed discussion. A final trap occurs when the study leaders turn into lecturers, nervously delivering sermons as they answer their own questions. Moreover, all of these styles compound the problem by tending toward studies which last too long. For example, an unwary leader or group depending too much on a study guide can find themselves answering up to twenty questions. (Some published guides are better than others in this respect. See Resource 8 for more on this.)

Having blasted this myth within a myth, I must offer a few qualifications. It is not good to go too far the other way and have only one person leading all the studies. A single mind and voice behind every study is dangerous, and allows a dominating style to become even more entrenched. This caution includes the group coordinator, who may not be gifted to lead studies anyway.

On the other hand, there should usually be two or three folks in an average group who are gifted to lead studies. Mature groups will discover who they are and appoint them as regular Bible study leaders. Now the process of finding these folks could certainly involve having several people in the group (who are willing and not coerced) try leading studies in the early phases of a group's life. In fact, this trial procedure could be part of a group's first contract. Groups must also be patient. Sometimes gifts take awhile to flower—people with obvious potential as study leaders can be allowed a few false starts. Furthermore, study leadership does not depend on innate gift alone but also learned skill. Therefore, conscious training (including courses outside the group), evaluation and feedback can all play a salutary role in the process of growing study leaders.

Finally, it is conceivable that a specialty group could gear itself specifically toward developing study leadership skills. Such a group would be an exception to the basic principle that every member of a group does not need to become a regular study leader.

Take Me to Your Leaders

I already hear the sighs of relief from people who are not able to lead studies and from groups who have suffered under their attempts. However, it is still critical to realize that no member is off the leadership hook. It is not enough to say that shared leadership does not consist only in sharing study-leading. The positive ideal must also be stated, namely, that every member is a leader in some sense. This is why the sentiment that more members should lead does not go far enough. In fact, *all* members should lead.

Actually, the idea of every member being a leader is true even in the beginning of a group. It all depends on how one defines leadership. A colleague of mine has collected dozens of definitions of leading. The one

I prefer goes like this—leadership means exercising one's gift to produce an effect on others. (Here I take gift to stand for everything that goes into making a person, including personality, background and spiritual gifts.) In a sense, then, members of a group have no option when it comes to leadership. As they express who they are, even in the first meeting, they are automatically leading. There is no such thing as a pure follower. Even someone with a very quiet personality produces an effect on other members and on the group as a whole.

The issues then are not whether or when people will lead, but how effective, active and progressive that leadership will be.

Effective leadership from each member depends on three things. First, it depends on the openness of the coordinator to expressions of leadership from others. The coordinator or designated "leader" can reduce the impact of another member by consistently cutting off that member. Sometimes this is very direct, such as interrupting anyone giving verbal leadership. Or they can simply ignore anyone who volunteers to do a job. In extreme cases, the coordinator might have a private chat with someone who they perceive as a competing leader. Usually members who receive such a caution do not last long. Stifled people will move on to a new situation where their contribution will be received.

The resistance of the coordinator can also be more subtle. Body language is a powerful communicator; some experts maintain that over ninety per cent of our messages are transmitted this way. A stiff, formal posture held by the coordinator does not invite input. Non-response also says a lot. I have seen group members reduced to silence when their contributions have received no feedback from the coordinator. Tightly organized meetings which follow a set pattern also inhibit member contributions. Finally, volunteerism can be squelched if coordinators manage to allow only token opportunities, or if they insist on being in charge of every process or project. Second-guessing every initiative will soon put a stop to those initiatives.

The second thing needed to promote effective shared leadership is a group full of members who have been trained in the principles of this book. If a group insists on the coordinator doing all of the leading, or if its definition of leadership is very narrow (being confined only to verbal gifts), then the effect of other members will be reduced rather than enhanced. A common example of this is the "leadership" exercised by members who show up to meetings irregularly or tardily. At first sight, this does not look much like leadership. It is easy for a group to ignore such behavior, or simply be quietly frustrated, but it would not be wise to leave it at that. In fact, inconsistent or inconsiderate attendance is often a sign of passive (and often unconscious) complaint about bad group dynamics. Finding out why members are not showing up to meetings (that is, finding out what their "leadership" expression means), can be very revealing and helpful. Remember, leadership must be received in order for it to be effective.

Lastly, effective leadership is integrated leadership. Members need to see their contributions as complementary. In the middle of a Bible study, a group should be prepared to allow pastoral or prayer gifts to be exercised. Sometimes the best thing that could happen to a Bible study is to stop and thank God for some truth he has revealed in his Word. A group needs to realize that different gifts reinforce one another. For example, someone who is good at drawing others out personally is an invaluable ally for someone who knows how to discover Bible truth. The same can be said for someone who can apply the text to concrete mission plans. Effective leaders glory in their diversity and make an effort to work together.

Checking Your Group Attitudes

Active leadership from each member also depends on various group attitudes being in place. The first thing to check is whether or not the group is afraid of active leadership. The kinds of passive leadership described above (being silent, arriving late) are less threatening because they are more easily ignored or explained away. Actually, there is nothing wrong with passive leadership and, to paraphrase Jesus, the passive will always be with you.

Mature groups, however, should move beyond the passive or the haphazard to a place where every member takes more direct responsibility and authority. In order for this to happen, groups must be committed to developing a deep understanding of each member's personality, experience and spiritual gifting. Each member needs to become conscious, comfortable and confident with regard to the gift of who they are. This is the basis for becoming active in leadership, that is, open to risking initiative. The best way to recognize and confirm the gift is not through books or workshops, prophecy or psychological inventories, but simply through trial and error. Here are seven guidelines for the sort of group atmosphere which is conducive to the process:

1. There is freedom in the group to fail, and to be trusted again when the failure was merely missed potential due to inexperience rather than a sign of no ability.

2. The schedule is not so tightly planned that no freedom exists to be spontaneous. Worship leaders can start up a song; pastors can interrupt the flow to concentrate on a personal need that they have perceived.

3. On the other hand, there is enough planning and discipline so that members can consistently exercise their particular muscles. For example, study leaders should not be struggling to get the Bible open before 9:30 p.m., and prayer should not always be crowded into the last ten minutes.

4. Members are allowed to concentrate on areas of leadership where they are comfortable. They are not required to be generalists or to switch leadership jobs from meeting to meeting.

5. But there will be gentle skepticism when it comes to any member's self-declaration of talent or spiritual gift—let them demonstrate it gradually before being appointed to a permanent role.

6. Coordinators should create room for the active involvement of others by boldly declaring that their job description does not encompass every task and then making sure that they leave some things undone. In my experience, groups always rise to the challenge of a leadership hole.

7. Finally, both coordinator and group should affirm members at every turn, and especially those with leadership roles that are more modest and behind-the-scenes (see 1 Cor 12:21-26). The encouragement can be verbal, such as expressions of appreciation, or practical, such as sending folks for special training.

In a word, an atmosphere of freedom gives room for active leadership to grow. Instead of a particular disgruntled member starting to attend irregularly, there is room in the agenda for them to regularly discuss their concerns about group dynamics, and room in the collective heart of the group to hear constructive criticism. One never knows, that complainer could turn out to be a natural expert at analyzing social dynamics, and thus a real asset to the group later on.

Developing Group Leadership
Progressive leadership refers to the goal of having members develop in their expressions of leadership during the life span of the group. During exploration, or the early meetings of a new group, the coordinator must take the most the initiative. However, in spite of the coordinator's preeminent role as a facilitator during the contracting process, and as a model during exploratory personal sharing, leadership contributions from each member are occurring as well. In a good group, each member should help shape the contract, and each member should begin to share from the first meeting. Furthermore, coordinators could also delegate leadership responsibilities from the very first meeting, for symbolic reasons if for nothing else.

A sign that the group is moving into the next stage, transition, is when the pace and power of member contributions increase, and when they begin to come without the coordinator asking. One sign for me which indicates that the hard work of transition has arrived is when group members begin to hold me to my promises: "Hey, you said we were going to end by 9:30 p.m. It's now 10:15! What gives?" More likely is the case where the complaint remains secret and the member who feels betrayed simply does not show up at the next meeting. Also there are those who play the contract-reminder role. Or the tension-relieving role (commonly called joking around). And especially the reality-testing role when it is directed at bringing the coordinator (me) back to earth. All of these roles, and many others identified by group researchers, begin to surface during transition.

I have to admit that as a leader I am tempted to let some of these roles annoy me. However, what should my first reaction be? (or at least my second reaction?) Gratitude that the group is beginning to mature, and my job is about to get easier as the members become active allies. This is where insecure coordinators can severely dampen progressive leadership. Unless they realize that complaints directed at them are natural and normal, they can become surly and defensive. What they should do instead is grow a thick skin and praise God that the group is beginning to make a very important statement: "This is our group, and we want to shape it together."

These group process roles, such as encourager and skeptic, are extremely important indicators of gifts and, thus, of future leadership positions. One should not jump to conclusions, however, because the roles played by any particular member can vary from meeting to meeting and even within one meeting. I have a friend who is an excellent facilitator of group process, but he turns into a tension-reliever when someone else is trying to chair a meeting. However, in spite of this flux, a pattern will emerge over time of the sort of role that fits each member best.

Coordinators should therefore watch and encourage this role-playing, and even dare to point it out in evaluation sessions involving the whole group. It can be a lot of fun. One approach would be to identify each member with the character of one of the eleven apostles (optimistically assuming that a Judas has not slipped into the group).

Transition in groups is hard work for coordinators as they receive the full brunt of member muscles being exercised. In this it parallels the notorious transition phase during labor just prior to delivering a baby. I have witnessed this phase of labor three times, up close and personal. In groups, as with labor, the result is worth it. A new level of honesty and the prospect of becoming a true group are on the way.

Some groups never make it past the exploratory honeymoon of polite conversation. To prevent this, coordinators can sometimes precipitate transition.

I will never forget the evening when I finally got up the courage to risk telling my group—especially the male members—that I was not feeling particularly supported in my position as coordinator. I felt that my contributions were being resisted and even ridiculed rather than respected, which made me doubt my mandate to coordinate. Because I was beginning to take my frustration over the situation out on my wife, I offered to step down. I suspected that a transitional meeting, reaching a new level of honesty, would result.

I was right, but I also catalyzed a painful process which ended in an unexpected way. A deeper problem in the group was revealed, namely, that the competition between the men in the group was producing a climate where the women were getting little or no chance to contribute. My hurt feelings paled in comparison to their frustration. We resolved to correct the situation, and a new contract resulted which effectively broadened the leadership base. A "shut-up clause" (pertaining to the men) featured prominently.

The openness won in transition extends to a new recognition and acceptance of the leadership of every member. The group then moves into the action stage of its life. This should be the longest stage, and it should be marked by full involvement of the gift of each member in order to achieve the goals of the group. The initiative required by the coordinator is greatly reduced.

Termination comes at the point where the group has achieved its set of goals, or become exhausted in the process. The group may decide to re-contract and continue or to end. In the first case, members often come and go. The group will go through exploration again as it sets new goals and possibly welcomes and incorporates new members. Therefore, the coordinator must be prepared to rise to the occasion and once more give shape to the process. The initiative required of the leader is even greater in the second case—when the group is ending altogether. As we have seen, groups usually resist ending well. Coordinators must help them say good-by.

And so we see that saying more members should be leaders does not refer to just some members but to all members. If Martians were to visit your group and ask to be taken to your leader, they should end up meeting everyone!

Group Leadership Is Best

It is not enough to leave behind the simple rotation of study leadership in favor of diverse and developed leadership by every member. For this still leaves the possibility of only seeing a group as a collection of gifted individuals placed like cogs in a machine dictated by laws of group dynamics. However, a true group is more organic than organized. The result is leadership by the whole group.

The whole group studies a passage of Scripture. The whole group shepherds each member. Pastors in the group may take a lead, but every member provides some kind of support to a hurting member. If one member suffers, every member does (1 Cor 12:26). This mutuality of experience produces a mutuality of responsibility. The same can be said of worship and mission leadership.

This philosophy of leadership may seem too subtle to be important, but the impact is real.

Synergism is the phenomenon where the combined effect of constituent elements in a system is greater than the sum of their individual effects. Groups at their best are synergistic systems. This is seen most easily in the beauty of Bible study with a group, where the insights are deeper and better applied than all the insights of individual students added together. Or imagine the impact of ten people visiting a needy person one at a time, and then compare it to the impact of that person being invited into a group of ten gifted friends.

The synergism of groups is not automatic. There is one critical prerequisite—humility. A humility which allows the coordinator to step aside and let the Spirit take over, trusting God and his capacity to work through his people harmoniously. A humility on the part of the members so that a climate of cooperation can grow rather than one of competition. And a humility expressed by the whole group as it expects the unexpected: members being inspired to express leadership beyond their usual roles and their formal positions. Under the Spirit, gifts can become enhanced and extended through the life of the group.

CHAPTER 6

• • • • •

MYTH #6

Good groups
are
polite

*Well I haven't actually died to sin, but I did
feel kind of faint once!*

Remember Sally's group which was introduced in chapter one? It looked good. There was a mission project in progress, people sharing the Bible study leadership, gifts being drawn out, a terminal contract in place, plans being made for future groups. But it did not start out that way.

In the early stages, it was almost like a different group. The meetings seemed very quiet and even dull. Sally did a lot more talking, and the other members did a lot more listening. The studies were very orderly—questions "from the book," followed by single answers. No one shared much, and when they did, it never made anyone feel uncomfortable. The singing was dutiful, but not very enthusiastic. There never were any hard probing questions like, "How is your personal witness going?" In short, Sally's group started out polite, and only later did it become good 'n' impolite.

How is it possible to claim impoliteness as a group quality?

Disenchanted Evenings

Polite groups are set up to maintain a certain unhealthy pattern, and no one, including the coordinator, ever rocks the boat. The same people are always right. The meeting always starts late and ends late, or there is a new person to introduce into the group each time. One person's chronic problem dominates every discussion. No one ever says, "Hey! We need to change how we do things!" The controlled frustration that results can become very tiresome.

I visited a group once, arriving a little late (I guess I was part of the problem). I noticed a heavy tone in the room right away. The study leader was already well into his presentation. Unfortunately, that is exactly what it was—a presentation. And, worse, it had little to do with a passage of Scripture. Instead, his monolog was entirely concerned with interpreting a personal dilemma he was going through. He droned on and on. Several others sat in a circle, slumped in chairs, immobile, eyes glazing over, not saying a single word.

At last I had to do something. I literally stopped the leader in mid-sentence and challenged his latest rationalization. Not harshly, but gently, with a question: "Do you think there might be another explanation?"

Instantly, the group's mood seem to switch. People sat forward, poised for the leader's answer. Several then started to ask questions themselves, probing, suggesting alternative points of view, calling him to accountability. Remarkably, we then moved on to other agendas altogether.

I think I may have upset the leader a little. But, to quote Mr. Spock of *Star Trek* fame, is it not better to sacrifice the one for the sake of the many? Some might have considered my interruption impolite, daring, dangerous. But it was not as risky as a group coma.

Ruts are killers. You may have heard the saying, "Ruts are graves with both ends pushed out." Any recurring pattern can introduce boredom.

Groups grow tired of hearing the same thing from the same person every meeting or the same kind of thing from different members. Groups long to go deeper, beyond superficial sharing. Groups also want to go beyond no sharing—silent members can distract a group because silence draws a lot of attention. The other members wonder: Have we upset these guys? Are they secretly judging us? Are they needy? How can we draw them out? Unprepared study leaders are also particularly harmful. Among other things, they can often end up moving through a passage at a funeral pace. Or their disorganization allows minds to wander. It is also bad when worship only consists of singing (off-key) and prayer always consists of going-around-the-circle in King James language. Furthermore, if these different components always occur in the same order, the group can become sleepy. For example, if the standard liturgy is chit-chat, followed by an opening prayer, three songs, then the study, followed by more sharing and prayer and, at the end, refreshments, then by the third meeting people will be getting restless. On the other hand, groups must also guard against being too novel. Some familiarity with the program allows members to concentrate on God and on one another rather than on guessing what will happen next.

The tragic thing is not the boredom factor itself. The real problem is that boring, polite meetings generally are not very effective, and because the group is not succeeding, it could suffer a premature death. The cause can be attributed to an individual leader (homicide), but it is more usually the fault of the whole group (suicide).

The Clark Kent Syndrome
Where do mild-mannered groups come from? Some of the causes of boredom we have already outlined in previous chapters. Groups that have gone on too long, even if they once had exciting meetings, can degenerate into bad patterns once they have accomplished their goals. Groups with frequent new members (or even just the threat of new members) will find it difficult to grow deep in sharing. Groups that are too large will still try to accomplish everything (making meetings too long) or they will consistently neglect certain folks—either way someone is going to feel alienated. Tyranny or oligarchy (decisions by a few) can wipe out the kind of democracy that makes a group interesting. Other contributing factors include:

Laws of Group Dynamics. Inertia will keep a group going in the same unhealthy direction unless some active intervention occurs. Further, the idea of entropy suggests that things will go from bad to worse unless energy is applied. In meetings, this means leaders must interrupt and try to correct unhelpful dynamics. In its overall life, a group must honestly and thoroughly evaluate how it is doing from time to time. Unfortunately, neither interruptions nor evaluations are natural or popular with most groups. No one wants to upset anyone.

Secret Things Have Power. We fear openness about our feelings, especially when they are negative. We are afraid that people will run away, or that a good thing will be spoiled. But the sad truth is that hidden feelings are not a good thing, and they only return to haunt us and the whole group. In my experience, honest confession about a hurt or frustration, when delivered with lots of "I" statements and no accusatory tone, produces good things in group life. We especially need to take a chance when one person is acting like a bottleneck, holding up the group. Someone in the group needs to confront that person lovingly.

Therapy Theory. Some people labor under the misunderstanding that basic nurture groups are meant to be therapy groups, able to confront deep psychological and spiritual problems. Groups can try to rise to the occasion, but they will soon exhaust themselves and turn off members who are less persistent. Furthermore, the profoundly needy will not be helped. Waves of sympathy or even codependency will wash uselessly against them to no effect.

Real therapy groups, on the other hand, must be led by trained and skilled counselors, and joined by members who know why they are there. Other groups should know how and where to refer needy folks for supplementary counseling or, conversely, how to act as allies alongside those offering professional treatment. Even groups that specialize in taking in people with "broken wings" (I have known such groups) must always differentiate between being therapeutic and offering therapy.

Imbalancing Act. Groups can fall into pits which force them to look in only one direction, and consequently their life can become stilted and dull. One such trap is to allow a single component of group life to take over. A typical case is when nurture dominates, usually in the form of Bible study. The message is given to members that only Bible study is important.

Bible study *is* important for most small groups, but it is not the only important component of group life. I recommend not calling small groups "Bible studies" because otherwise there is an uphill battle from the start to introduce other components like fellowship, worship and mission. Aside from watching terminology, the group can also avoid imbalance through good contracting, careful planning of each meeting and periodic reviews. For example, groups focusing on prayer or support or ministry for awhile must be honest enough to ask, "Are we missing something by not having a more systematic Bible study?"

Compatibility Conjecture. Some groups make the mistake of trying to constitute their membership to only include compatible people. In fact, the whole point of good group life is to discover how unlovely your fellow members are, at the same time as they are discovering the same thing about you. The most carefully contrived membership always includes people that will rub you the wrong way and therefore leads to growth on your part. If a group attempts to maintain a status quo of compatibility and comfort, it usually only succeeds in keeping out some interesting gifts that could be a great help later when the group starts to fight.

Good Things Come in Strange Packages. One way of thinking about gifts is in three large categories: princely gifts (focusing on plans and managing), priestly gifts (focusing on people and pastoring), and prophetic gifts (focusing on principles and teaching). The last gift in particular can be neglected in a group that seeks calmness. Prophets like to poke holes in unworkable plans and sentimental care. Recently, I added a prophetic type to a small management team, someone who was not actually going to do very much. Her brief role was to cause trouble. This can seem like a nuisance to planning types who just want to get things done. But wisdom and alternative perspectives are critical to good planning, as well as other group processes.

Groups should always value and seek a range of leadership gifts. It makes life more interesting. If you are not convinced, just read the chapter on "deviance" in Em Griffin's *Getting Together*. I especially like how he describes the disciples: "If [Jesus] could put up with a political fanatic (Simon the Zealot), a pair of emotional hotheads nicknamed the Sons of Thunder (James and John), a man who openly questioned his resurrection (Thomas), a corrupt tax collector (Matthew) and a money grabber who betrayed him (Judas), how can we do less? In the long run it turned out to be a pretty good group."

Jesus, Meek and Mild?

A final factor producing humdrum groups is a false spirituality derived from a false picture of how Jesus handled his famous group. Even if people accept that Jesus might have had a closed group, they persist in the idea that he was very nice in that group. Of course, a quick look at the Gospels shows that nothing could be further from the truth. Just consider these episodes from Matthew:

- [ ] 8:21-22. Jesus sets a disciplined contract.
- [ ] 8:26. Jesus probes hearts.
- [ ] 9:37-38. Jesus challenges toward mission.
- [ ] 10:1. Jesus gives real responsibility and authority.
- [ ] 10:2-4. Jesus risks including the incompatible.
- [ ] 10:5-16. Jesus counts the cost.
- [ ] 12:48-50. Jesus confirms the contract.
- [ ] 14:16, 27. Jesus encourages faith overcoming fear.
- [ ] 16:15. Jesus asks direct questions.
- [ ] 16:21. Jesus does not avoid the hard truth.
- [ ] 16:23. Jesus rebukes.
- [ ] 16:24-28. Jesus deepens the contract.
- [ ] 17:20. Jesus is honest.
- [ ] 17:22-23. Jesus risks emotion.
- [ ] 20:20-24. Jesus allows people to hang themselves (not Judas).
- [ ] 24:25. Jesus warns.
- [ ] 26:10. Jesus protects the weak.
- [ ] 26:31. Jesus says the worst.
- [ ] 26:36-39. Jesus shows deep feeling.
- [ ] 26:40. Jesus asks pointed questions.
- [ ] 28:18-20. Jesus extends trust after failure.

We need to leave behind any suggestion that being in a group with Jesus was a comfortable exercise. Jesus was always respectful, but he was not always "polite."

Thriving on Chaos

Two words that appeared in the above list describing Jesus as a small group leader were *fear* and *risk*. Groups are afraid to risk impoliteness. They are afraid primarily of the chaos that will result. Bible studies verging on heresy. Sharing that is too raw. Worship gone wild. Mission into uncharted territory. So the tendency is to keep the lid on, to keep control. This is unfortunate, for groups can control themselves to death.

Like the therapist in the great movie, *Ordinary People*, I don't have much regard for maintaining control. Groups need to replace inhibition with inspiration from the recent management book, *Thriving on Chaos*. The basis of chaos in this context is not disorder and randomness, but an environment where individual contributions are encouraged even when the outcome is not fully known. The group process is not completely controlled, but there is faith that good things will come out in the end (though we are not sure exactly what those things will be). Now if secular management experts are advocating this approach to running corporations, how much more should we embrace it when we know that God is superintending our groups? We need to trust God more as we trust his people. It is a special tragedy when the Bible study component of groups is boring. For example, we described the problem of never rotating the study leadership or rotating it inappropriately. Here are ten other sub-myths about Bible study to avoid:

1. Groups must always do Bible study. Actually, there are sources of nurture other than Bible study, such as studying books or articles, sermon debriefing, meditation on a hymn, using records, tapes, or video, book reports, testimonies, attending workshops together, and mini-lectures from members. Taking a brief break from Bible study can be good for a group, and good for future group study.

2. Groups must always do systematic, inductive study. Again, variety is the spice of small group life. Roberta Hestenes describes twenty different study methods in *Using the Bible in Groups.* Only six of them are systematic.

3. Groups doing discussion study will inevitably fall into a whirlpool of ignorance that leads down into a hole of heresy. My simple answer is that I have not seen this to be true. In fact, just the opposite can be found in history; most heresy has arisen in a little room with one person trying to understand Scripture or formulate doctrine alone. The work the Holy Spirit is meant to do is to come among people gathered in Jesus' name and remind them of his words. Do we believe this? If we do, then groups should be seen as a marvelous safeguard against heresy.

4. Lecturing by one leader is more efficient and safer than discussion. In a way this is true, especially for those who believe the myth about heresy. However, the cost of protecting against wrong ideas or a winding path to the truth is too high. Misguided notions put forward by members will not necessarily kill a group, but listening to one lecturer will.

5. You are supposed to follow directions in the study guide. I like to say that choosing a study guide is less important than losing a study guide. What I mean is that guides are just that—guides, and not blueprints. They do not need to be followed to the letter. To guard against this tendency when leading, study the passage yourself before turning to the guide. Then use the guide to selectively augment your questions. Finally, take your study plan to the group rather than having the guidebook open. The last thing you need during a good discussion is for someone to interrupt and say, "Hey, we missed question number three!"

6. Good Bible studies will be long and intense. Or, the more Scripture you study, and the more points you get out of it, the better. There is such a thing as too much study. There might be too many Bible truths generated to remember, let alone to apply during the week. A good Bible study discussion zeroes in on one point. Only a few carefully crafted questions are needed to expose this point. To aid the process, study a short passage of Scripture. For example, a whole chapter of a Pauline letter is usually too much for a group to swallow in one meeting. When a group is not disciplined about its study time, then other components of group life get crowded out. A group does not live by bread (nurture) alone. A smart group will try to build some good sharing, worship and challenge around the Bible truth discovered in each meeting.

7. People come prepared and eager to study. I assume just the opposite, that members come into a group meeting very distracted by the pressures and pleasures of everyday life. I want to get their attention. At the start of the study, this means having an introduction which generates interest, and using a "hook" question to personally engage folks in the theme (see IVP's Lifeguide Bible Studies for examples of introductions and hooks). It also means the study leader has to model animation, enthusiasm and, if possible, a sense of humor. Stiff leaders stifle the steam of the group. As the study progresses, do introduce variety into how the discussion is "blocked." Do not move from an observation question on a verse, to an interpretation question, to an application question, and then repeat the process on the next verse, and the same on the verse after that. A single, predictable rhythm will be tiresome. Explore an observation more fully. Ask more than one interpretation question in a row. Follow an application with prayer right in the middle of the study. Keep the members guessing and they will keep awake.

8. Do not follow tangents. Almost all authors of books on leading Bible studies seem to be paranoid about tangents (that is, when someone makes a point or raises a question that is not on target with the planned aim of the study). I believe that this paranoia is misplaced, and that it leads to uptight leaders and uptight studies. As long as the passage under consideration is reasonable in length, the aim of the study is precise, the number of questions modest, there should be plenty of time to indulge a couple of tangents. My advice is to relax and not worry so much about it. In fact, I try to be glad that at least someone is interested in something, even if my aim has to be put on hold for a few minutes. Often, a tangent will be of general interest and actually help to raise the temperature of the meeting a little.

This is so valuable that if someone else does not tempt with a tangent, I might. For example, I like to ask deliberately provocative questions (where the group will probably not agree on an answer) before I ask the safer, sounder questions. To see what I mean, turn to Mark 3:13-19, on the appointing of the Twelve. The safe question would be, "Do you experience this same rhythm of the Twelve, that is, being with Jesus, and then being sent out to minister?" A dangerous question is, "Why were no women chosen?" Or "Why did Jesus, who knew Judas was going to betray him, still appoint him?" Whether by means of an opportunistic tangent or an open-ended question, I want folks sitting on the edge of their seats when we get to the true aim of the discussion.

9. Good Bible studies are orderly. What do I want to see when I visit discussions led by students from my class at Regent College? Energized, excited, engaged people. Interruptions, people talking at once. More than one person answering each question. People asking their own questions. People commenting on the answers given by other members. Lots of ideas flowing, but with a thread emerging, and a summary of the actual main result at the end. (Someone other than the leader should be able to offer this summary.) A sense of anticipation permeates the room as the members pray for power to apply the truth in the next week. In short, study leaders need to learn how to turn the humdrum into a hubbub.

10. Study leaders should prepare in depth. Often the battle for briefer studies is won in the leader's preparation. Leaders should prepare, but they should not overprepare. To spend hours in one's study getting ready to lead a study produces many temptations—too many aims, too many questions, too long an introduction, too many comments on background information, not enough focus on the text. The leader will have to struggle not to answer his or her own questions. A lack of spontaneity creeps in as members sense that the study details are predetermined, and the leaders resist learning anything they had not already thought of while preparing. Paradoxically, the study moves too quickly from question to question, but it also lasts too long. To stay open to their own sense of discovery, study leaders should probably limit their preparation to two hours maximum. Good study guides can help speed up preparation.

General Dynamics, Inc.

Other dynamics of group life also affect the boredom factor. For example, true sharing should be distinguished from superficial chit-chat. I have been in groups where the members spend a lot of time talking about themselves, but the topics do not range very broadly. To avoid this, topics for sharing need to be deliberately suggested, and they should move progressively deeper through the life span of the group. This again involves careful contracting. Sharing expected in the first contract should be fairly tame.

I remember being in a new group where one member (due to a bad experience) was extremely nervous about committing to psychological exercises and deep sharing. We made it clear that he would not be pushed beyond his comfort zone. Two years later, this same member asked the following question at the start of a meeting, "How do you feel about death, and what would you do if you only had a year to live?" Clearly, the trust and vulnerability level in the group had changed.

Basic groups should reach a phase where probing questions of accountability can be asked of each member. John Wesley's groups provide a model for such development, as we see in the following contract: "to desire some person among us to speak his own state first, and then to ask the rest, in order, as many and as searching questions as may be, concerning their state, sins, and temptations" (from *The Radical Wesley*).

As for worship, it is important to distinguish warm-up singing (to build fellowship) from true worship. In my opinion, one great truth ought to be established: Groups do not need to sing at all! Experimenting with a variety of methods of worship can be exciting, and a good antidote to boredom.

No gift should be forced on a group, including singing, speaking in tongues, prophecy, or healing prayer. Worship (along with these allied gifts) is one area where there is opportunity to practice being a true group. Be sensitive to the "weaker" brother or sister who is uncomfortable with a particular kind of worship. If you just must speak in tongues publicly, go to a group which is ready for this, or wait for your group to be ready.

Finally, it is a simple fact that members will grow tired of one another even in the best group. The best antidote, is also simple: an outward focus from the very start.

Some say that trouble-shooting is easy—if someone is troubling you, shoot 'em.

Unfortunately, it is not that simple. First, the problem is not always a person. In the case of default dynamics, a bad process just begins to happen. For example, in conversational prayer, you might start off, and then the person next to you prays, and then the person next to them, and so on in order around the circle. This can happen in spite of the directions you have given. Although a bit boring, it is not a big problem, that is, unless the people across from you have never prayed aloud before! They are feeling trapped and uncomfortable as their turn inexorably approaches. What should the facilitator do? Interrupt and pray again, thus breaking the pattern.

Some problems are even more delicate. For more on how to identify and handle common problems see Resources Five and Six.

Emily Post Revisited
It is true that some of my advice for quiet, polite groups that put up with

bad dynamics would cause Emily Post, or her modern incarnation, Miss Manners, to blanch in horror. Indeed, there are times when a bit of politeness and consideration in group life is particularly important.

For example, the facilitator may tolerate funny ideas, even heretical ideas, from a group member knowing that the group itself will correct untruth. However, it is important for the facilitator to protect the sensitive member from correction which is too aggressive. Heresy head-hunters should not be allowed to pounce on every tentative, but clearly unorthodox, remark and squash the speaker like a bug. The facilitator needs to step in and say, "Hey, let's give Sue an opportunity to explore what she said a bit more—to see if we heard it fully."

The same protective function extends to anyone who becomes a victim of meanness. Or even a victim of enthusiasm. Interruptions during heated or enthusiastic discussions are fine, and a sign of health, but they should be minimized when a person is sharing for the very first time. A simple, "Excuse me, I am not sure George was finished with what he was saying" will do the trick.

Further, while sharing in a group must deepen in order to avoid the doldrums, there is such a thing as premature honesty, sharing which is too much too soon. The first meeting is probably not the place to hear details about a suicide attempt or a messy family background, and it certainly is not a platform for one person to give a one-hour testimony. Facilitators need to be bold enough to slow sharing down to a reasonable pace. Good modeling and directions help, but sometimes the direct approach is needed: "Sorry, but I think we better save some of that for future meetings, when we have built a level of trust that allows your refreshing kind of honesty. Could we pray for you now, and then move on to the next person?"

Finally, although Bible studies should be marked by a hubbub, a spirited interchange, I mean guided chaos, not anarchy. The group should never lose sight of a certain level of respect. One way to remind members about the necessary respect is to establish and review ground rules for discussions. For example, the group will respect God (and the Scriptures when studying them), they will respect the facilitators (letting them exercise the general role assigned to them, as well as expressing their specific gift), and they will respect one another. Is it possible to have an animated exchange and still maintain this kind of respect? Yes.

CHAPTER 7

• • • • •

MYTH #7

Mission
must
wait

*"Remember the good ol' days when we'd just
give 'em a Gospel of John?"*

Mission, defined very broadly, is not an option for a Christian. It's a mandate. Every disciple is called to reach out to a lost and hurting world with the word and works of the gospel.

Small group mission does not arise spontaneously. Further, it does not always work. However, mission through groups is always worth the effort for the sake of obedience, and also because mission produces maturity. This runs counter to the mythology that maturity is a prerequisite of mission, or that groups need to wait before embracing and embarking on mission.

The School of Mission

A few years ago my wife and I coordinated a small group which had covenanted to plant a ministry presence on the eastside of our city. Like so many cities in the world, the eastside was the low-rent district of our city, exhibiting more crime, poverty and general misery than seen along the wide, tree-lined boulevards a few blocks west. It seemed in our minds to be a social and spiritual mission field, lacking resources and churches on the one hand, and offering cross-cultural challenges both economically and ethnically on the other.

What did we know about the philosophy and practice of urban ministry? Almost nothing. But the four couples and (later) two singles did have enthusiasm. We gathered for our meetings in a group home for teens on the eastside, and prayed. Some of the ladies worked in a family drop-in center in the area, put money aside, met with related ministries, studied a plan for employing the unemployed and running a small business, and looked at storefront property. Ultimately, however, we failed.

Not one of our plans bore any fruit. No storefront was rented. No business was started. The money we saved reverted to the general church budget, and the group disbanded.

What had we done wrong? Actually, nothing. We had a good contract which made it clear when we should give up, with dignity and friendships intact. We had a good balance of gifts. We did not ignore our internal relationships or personal growth. We did not wait to see if everything was in place before stepping out. The fact that our plan eventually lost steam was not a reflection on the way the group had been formed or run. It was simply not the right timing (and maybe not the right location) for the church or the individuals involved. The main lesson we learned was that it was okay for a group to try something and fail. In fact, the freedom to fail is critical to the life of a church or other organization which wants to be risky and reproductive, that is, seeing its life extended through new types of groups and new types of outreach.

Three years later some of the original group members, and a few others, actually rented a community center on Sunday afternoons and began to meet for a fellowship time centered on singing, teaching, eating and keeping kids involved. During the intervening years, two of the couples had begun an outreach Bible study which served as a lifeline to the gospel for four to five people who were at best half-converted and at worst very confused. Other relationships had been kept alive through friendly contacts, so it was not unnatural to find us trying something like a fellowship meeting. This lasted for only three months, and therefore could once again be seen as a failed experiment.

However, we made some significant advances over the previous mission experience. We actually worked together as a group in the real world, a real world which was significantly closer to the places that members actually lived in the city. Most of us could walk to the community center. Some had actually moved into the area to promote Christian networking. Friendships between children and adults were strengthened. A relationship with the community center was established. The following spring, we organized a tiny softball league with people in the neighborhood. The summer would bring hot-dog parties in the park, and conversations with other families in the vicinity. Babysitting was exchanged. We packed out a class on toddlers in a nearby health unit.

We were stumbling along and learning some lessons about how to bring Christ creatively and realistically into an area of the city, even if it was not the eastside!

Tending the Group Garden

The first lesson I learned with my friends is that mission does not emerge out of a vacuum. The mission component of a small group is like the wonderful fruit of a garden. You can fertilize and nourish the garden, weed and water, expose it to the power of the sun, and provide a stable network of stakes and string, but if "ya don't plant seeds ya won't get no beans!" Likewise, although the nurture, prayer, worship and community components of group life are essential from the start, the mission seed must also be planted in the earliest stages of a group, or mission will never come to fruition.

Often overheard at a group's first meeting is, "We need to get to know one another before we reach out," or "We need to find out what God wants us to do," or "We need to study what the mission possibilities are." Although this approach is all right up to a point, these sentiments can also lead to lots of inreach and no outreach. When mission is delayed over or prayed over too long, the ground of the group garden gets hard. This happens naturally and quickly as traditions get established, patterns get formed, expectations solidify and friendships take root.

Now there is nothing wrong with group identity and closeness. These are desirable and, in a good group, inevitable. But friendships and a sense of "we-ness" can become unhealthy if not balanced by outreach. The problem with plants stuck in one pot is that they become rootbound. A concern for those beyond the pot is essential to the growth of the group and the maturing of its members. As Elizabeth O'Connor of The Church of the Savior has put it, in healthy disciples the inward journey must be matched by the outward journey.

Who says?

Jesus. In his work with the disciples, and particularly the twelve apostles, Jesus demonstrated this balance between group identity and outreach. In fact, the two words usually used to describe Jesus' central followers capture this very duality of purpose, *disciple,* which means "learner" and *apostle,* which means "sent one." Here is how Mark summarizes the "contract" of the Twelve: "He appointed twelve—designating them apostles—that they might be with him and that he might send them out to preach and to have authority to drive out demons" (3:14-15). Note the balance of the group identity "with him" and group mission when "sent out." The inward journey in dialogue with the outward journey. Jesus knew that both of these were critical to leadership development and full expression of the kingdom.

But Jesus was very sophisticated in the development of the mission life of the Twelve. They were not recruited and thrown out into advanced ministry in the same day. Careful preparation and progress marked Jesus' method. This is described in classics like Robert Coleman's *The Master Plan of Evangelism* and A. B. Bruce's *The Training of the Twelve.*

Jesus knew that basic teaching and modeling (Mk 4—5) had to precede a personal mission project (Mk 6). He knew that sometimes the disciples needed to retreat (Mk 6:31) and sometimes they needed to be challenged to meet needs that landed in front of them (Mk 6:37). Jesus encouraged teamwork (Mk 6:38-43), trying in spite of risk of failure (Mk 9:18), learning from mistakes (Mk 9:28-29), and seeing the bigger picture of kingdom work (Mk 9:38-41; 10:13-16).

All along, Jesus taught the ultimate cost of mission, that is, laying down your life, but he did not make it personal until near the end (Mk 10:38; 13:9-13). Finally, after Jesus paid the full price of his mission, and then left bodily a second time, sending the Spirit in his stead, the disciples were ready to fulfill their marching orders and be dispersed permanently into their mission, whatever the cost. The rhythm of being together and reaching out was over for this group. Now they would each go out and establish new groups of disciples, and the pattern would begin again.

Ideas and Ideals

But what if you do not happen to be working with the disciples? Actually, your raw material might be even more promising! Remember what the twelve apostles started out like. Yet, no matter what group you are blessed with, you know your leadership does not measure up to that provided by Jesus. Should you give up now, or are there some simple principles to hold onto? In a word, yes.

1. Mission does not develop automatically. Contract for mission as you would any other component of group life (such as Bible study and sharing). Discuss ideas, test feelings, establish plans—being as specific and realistic as possible for each phase of the group's life.

2. Do not fall into mission by coercion. Don't let a strong leader or member impose an outreach plan, such as having an evangelistic Bible study, onto a new group.

3. Do not fall into mission by default. A group may simply drift into a certain pattern of outreach without any discussion or agreement.

4. Later is too late. Introducing mission is like moving into a new neighborhood. If you do not meet your neighbors in the first month, it becomes almost impossible by the second. Groups, or at least group members inspired by their group, have to start meeting their "neighbors" meaningfully from the very start.

5. Do not be too ambitious. What is appropriate in the later phases of the group would not work well in the first meeting. A new group can easily build in some support for every member's personal witness, but planning for an evangelistic dinner party at the end of your first month together is probably premature. Someone could record intercession requests and answers from the start, but to appoint that person as a mission project coordinator would usually be too intimidating.

6. Mission should not remain static in a group. As with every other component of group life, it should grow naturally and be developed intentionally. The natural growth occurs as love and knowledge increase in the group. The seedbed of mission is compassion and gifting. As we love one another and recognize one another's gifts, love for the stranger and leadership in the world can take root. On the other hand, the group needs to intentionally stretch itself into new areas of mission, ones that require more risk and more teamwork, otherwise compassion and gift-expression inside the group can turn sour.

7. A particular group can only go so far in mission. One limit to growth is the policy of the church or organization to which the group belongs. Some church leaders may consciously or unconsciously resist the kind of diversity which arises when groups develop an independent sense of mission.

A more common obstacle is the fact that nurture groups do not as a rule become mission groups. (By "mission group" I mean the kinds of groups developed at The Church of the Savior in Washington, D.C.—a group of people whose raison d'etre is an outreach objective.) For the mission group, other components of life together (study, sharing and worship) exist to serve the main mission objective. I believe that being in this kind of group at different times in our lives is important for maturing as disciples, but such groups also depend on a certain amount of mature discipline from its members from the start. So mission groups are not for everybody at every stage. In particular, it is unlikely that the miscellaneous collection of gifts and visions that emerges during the growth of a basic nurture group will ever mesh automatically into such a single-minded mission goal. Thus, basic groups should come to a natural end where members, either individually or in clusters, move off to form or join mission groups.

In a sense, the mission groups which founded the church arose because of an eruption planned by Jesus and a harmony inspired by the Spirit. We call it Pentecost.

What Shall We Then Do?

But there was plenty of mission going on before Pentecost. You do not just get into a Volkswagen Beetle group and then long wistfully for outreach, perhaps wearing a bumper sticker that says, "I have a Cadillac mission group inside me fighting to get out." Every group, and every member of every group, needs to be challenged to think outwardly, pray outwardly and reach outwardly. From the very start. At every stage.

A basic nurture group can begin very simply, putting in its contract a commitment to personal witness. This should produce a regular reminder to each member about key folks they are exposing to the gospel. Or should be exposing to the gospel. Such a clause would cover relatives, neighbors and colleagues. You might call it the "Aunt Sally" clause for short.

The Aunt Sally clause might include the "prayer of opportunity," praying that God would give you an opening to share the love of Jesus in word and deed in the next seven days. Such a clause is suitable for new Christians and veteran disciples, but they should only pray if they mean it! God seems to delight in providing such encounters.

A beginning group can make a commitment to support members in their work (whether it be in a home, in the office or at school) by engaging ethical issues and encouraging creativity. This, too, is part of the general Christian mission, traceable to the Genesis mandate to till the earth and tend the garden.

From the start a group could incorporate intercessory prayer for concerns beyond the group. These could be particular concerns raised by the members, or one or more regular focal points (a particular ministry in the church or an issue in society). The group members could have a cycle of intercession rotating between their local church, their city, their government leaders and their foreign mission concerns. Someone could record prayers and, where known, answers.

Most basic groups should be able to handle a one-time project by the end of their first year. A favorite is the evangelistic dinner party, where friends are invited to a good meal or dessert reception and then exposed to Jesus through some speaker who is adept at making the non-churched feel at home and the Bible seem relevant. A good time of year to hold a party like this is during Christmas and Easter when folks are more open to religious things. Suitable speakers for such events are available in every locale—just ask around.

Other one-time projects include hosting a social event for the church, helping out with a hospital or nursing home service, visiting a rescue mission, sponsoring a foreign student, raising money for a special need inside or outside the church, joining a day-camp team, and running a work party at the home of a shut-in. Almost anything that gets the group "outside of itself" will do at this stage.

After this, if it has not already happened, the group should move conceptually from the simple to the subtle in terms of mission. Begin planting the idea of budding off new groups at the end of the group's life.

By its second year together most basic groups should be ready for a sustained, but still limited, project. Such projects will take a reasonable amount of time inside and outside of group meetings. However, they do not need to be the main focus of the group (in fact, it is not necessary for every member to be equally involved). Examples include regularly staffing the visitors' center in your church, adopting one of the church's local or foreign missionaries, coordinating food-bank collections, sponsoring a refugee, and putting on a regular dinner in a downtown youth center.

Finally, a nurture group which makes it to the second or third year and is still healthy should begin to think about inserting a volcano clause into its contract. Be specific about the eruption date. Begin to plan and pray toward it.

Skimming the Book of Acts, I am struck by the range of mission and mission groups found there. For more on the variety of possibilities see

Resource Seven. The rationale for the categories found there is clear—the dynamics of each type of mission group are quite different, and therefore the commitment, leadership and support structures needed vary from type to type. However, no matter how clever your program is, remember there are always exceptions.

For example, I know a group whose core has been together for half my lifetime (sixteen years), whose membership has frequently been too large for a healthy nurture group, whose mission focus is too diffuse to qualify as a mission group (over the years the group has been involved with refugee work, missionary support, prison outreach and ministry to the handicapped), and whose ex-members refuse to be "ex." People remain so attached to the life of this group, even when they move overseas, that they treat it as a home away from home when back in town. They have forced me to invent a new type of membership, the associate member. Recently, their annual "reunion" picnic drew fifty or sixty members and guests.

Why has this group remained so vital? Simply because of its radical commitment to mission. Does it fit into any of the mission group categories I suggest in Resource Seven? No. In fact, it is probably a house church, or the nucleus of a new church, and not a group at all—but this still shows that categories need to be handled carefully.

No matter what may differentiate the various mission groups, much more links them together. The following qualifications are true of most mission groups:

1. Mission groups will have an extremely clear and precise contract. The members need to know when they have accomplished their task, when to change strategies, and when to give up.

2. Although members will sustain other dimensions of group life (such as study and sharing), planning and performing the mission will take up a large amount of time. Often the group will not meet weekly; sometimes they will not get together for basic group interaction more than monthly.

3. Mission groups can last longer and grow larger than basic nurture groups. They can keep going and keep growing as long as the commitment to a clear mission purpose keeps them healthy. Of course, periodic reviews and recommitments are essential, as well as sub-groupings once the membership exceeds 15-20. Some mission groups may end up as new churches.

4. Although formed to serve a purpose, mission groups cannot move into action immediately. They still must build relationships between members through the early stages of group life. This is what separates mission groups from committees and task forces.

5. However, early stages of interpersonal growth, and any planning for the project, should be as brief as possible. Too long a delay in action can be deadly (for example, when an evangelistic Bible study never manages to attract a non-Christian because the Christian members become too churchy). In a sense, it is better to not officially declare yourself to be a mission group until the mission is under way.

6. There is more opportunity and necessity for specialists being appointed in mission groups than in other types of groups.

7. Mission is not restricted to mature people, but mission groups generally are.

What's Happening?
The life of the collection of friends I described at the start of this chapter continues to percolate. Lately, my wife and I have been in a single focus support group, specifically one aimed at the survival of new parents who did not know that it is okay to put six-month-old babies to bed when you think they should go to bed, not just when they look tired. (Our oldest daughter partied till 3:00 a.m. on her first New Year's Eve.)

Does our current group sound too cozy and introspective? How do we reconcile being in a mere support group with our earlier enthusiasm for action in the wider world?

First, we realize that "ya gotta do what ya gotta do." There are rhythms in life. As the author of Ecclesiastes might say, "There is a time for support and a time for action." New parents need all the help they can give one another, especially in a society offering so little tangible support for families. Sometimes there is little energy left for anything else besides parenting. In fact, our group could only find time to meet every second week. God understands: he invented kids.

Second, though not laboring under false guilt, our group has never been an island unto itself. We have been involved with the full range of mission-mindedness described above. We adopted a missionary couple from the start (and, incidentally, prayed with them as they adopted two kids in Thailand). We hosted a couples' event at our church. We invited a single parent to join our group. We even prayed for a couple outside the group to get pregnant. For a long time there were no results, but we kept praying, and finally, they did get pregnant. They now have a beautiful son.

Third, all things pass. Our initial panic as parents has abated. We are preparing to move to a long-term format, meeting once a month or even less often and sustaining friendships informally during intervening weeks. This will give us time to take on new projects separately or together. In fact, almost the whole group is intimately involved at various levels with a revamped preschool ministry at the church.

Only two couples in this most recent group incarnation can be traced back to the original eastside mission. But the eastside mission group itself is still bonded together by having worked together and failed together. We had a reunion last month. Actually, it was a bittersweet occasion, as just two weeks earlier we had suffered with one of the couples who lost a baby to Sudden Infant Death Syndrome. Recently, another eastside wife called to say that her husband was in the hospital for exploratory surgery. And several folks from our current group, and one from the fellowship experiment in the community center, have bought a cabin together.

The best news of all is that an eastside mission has finally been launched by our church. There have been outreach meetings for a year. A kids club is the focus right now, with a couple of dozen neighborhood children from many cultural backgrounds involved. And yes, two couples from our original mission group have been part of the launch. One of my favorite experiences with this program was meeting some Hindu boys and their father (warrior caste) and inviting them to the club. My oldest daughter was with me. I wonder what mission she will be part of in the future.

So you see, we are all still good friends, in spite of trial and tragedy, able to laugh at our early attempts at doing something for the kingdom. I am glad we did not wait before embracing mission.

RESOURCES
• • • • •

Resource 1
Contracting

There is great value in the process of group contracting or covenanting. In fact, the process is in many ways more valuable than the product. The groups I have been part of have rarely referred to their contract once it has been set, except perhaps at the end of a cycle!

By Any Other Name

Some people prefer to call the group agreement a covenant, thinking it sounds more biblical and more friendly. However, biblical covenants were unilateral (God usually formulated and offered them), and they were frequently broken. The idea of a contract, though sounding more business-like and less friendly, might be a better description of both the process and result of setting a group agenda. For example, group contracting usually involves negotiation, careful definition of terms, and lots of fine print.

Whatever the label chosen, covenant or contract, I know that some people are still uncomfortable with the concept. They either have had good experiences without an explicit group agreement or bad experiences with one. Yet every group does have an agenda which gets expressed primarily in the shape of its meetings. The question is really whether every member feels happy with the purpose and activities, that is, whether the purpose and activities are optimal for the group. The only way to find out for sure is to talk about it, getting the dreams, expectations and planned contributions of each member out in the open. Then clarifications and compromises begin until a consensus is achieved. This group-building discussion is the best result of contracting, not so much the draft agreement itself. In fact, few groups refer to their contract except when evaluating at the end of a phase and setting a new course.

The problems with not having an explicit agreement fall into three categories: (a) the group is not clear when it is succeeding; (b) the group is not clear when and how to deepen its life; and (c) the group never knows when it has succeeded and therefore when it is time to end. Furthermore, not taking enough time on contracting can lead to vague agreements that are not very satisfying, or to imposed or assumed contracts that are secretly frustrating for some members.

Do you have to have a contract to have a good group experience? No, but a contract might make the experience even better.

What about people who have had bad experiences with contracting? All I can suggest is that the process was not well handled, for I am convinced that contracts are the key to healthy groups. I have learned this the hard way. Whenever I consult with a group in trouble, the problem invariably relates to poor contracting.

Setting Goals

The goals of contracting are:

☐ to learn more about each member's expectations and possible contributions.

☐ to hear what God might have in mind for the group.

☐ to come to some agreement as to the overall purpose of the group and the specific activities that will serve that purpose.

☐ to allow people who do not feel comfortable with the profile and program of the group to leave before the group really even starts.

☐ to allow others to join as the nature of the group becomes clear.

☐ to start in earnest around the agreed agenda, with a sense of commitment to the contract.

☐ to have some idea when the group has accomplished its aim, or needs to re-aim.

Getting Started

1. Talk. At the beginning, some groups balk at talk. They are anxious to get started, to get the group functioning. While it is true that the official beginning can be delayed too long (so that people become bored or discouraged), it is good to spend at least a couple of meetings to set a contract. This does not seem like too great an investment for what might end up as a two-or-three-year experience.

Contracting easily doubles as a great opportunity to learn a lot about each member right from the start. Let the conversation be as open-ended as possible. The facilitator can ask broad questions like: What do you hope to gain from the group? What can you contribute? How will we know when we are done? (This last question—talking about ending—can seem a bit depressing, but actually can take on a positive tone of anticipation.) Once a general purpose is established, move on to specific strategies (for example, what kind of Bible study, whether to have prayer partners, the possibility of singing). Avoid getting into logistics (where and when to meet, coffee before or after) too early. In my experience, the most insurmountable problems are quickly solved once there is actually a commitment to be a group.

Who should answer all of the questions? Every potential member of the group.

What topics are open for consideration? Every item that comes up, from the sublime (controversial spiritual gifts) to the mundane (handling tardiness).

Someone should act as a secretary and record the comments during the contracting session. That person, or someone else with the gift of deciphering notes and producing summaries, should collate the results and circulate them between meetings.

2. Pray. Start the meeting with prayer, recognizing that contracting is a spiritual process. After the first meeting, the contract will be rough, and probably include some competing or unclear goals. Each member should pray that God would give some direction during the upcoming finalization.

3. Negotiate. This is the right word for what needs to happen as a compromise is reached. The main reason Bob wants to be in a group is that he wants to study in depth. Sue on the other hand is very keen on building friendships. So the middle ground is proposed: a disciplined study sometime in the first 75 minutes of most meetings, but lasting no longer than 45 minutes, leaving plenty of time for sharing and prayer. This is also the time to clarify terms. Do Bob and Sue mean the same thing by "Bible study"? Also point out any activities proposed which do not directly serve the group purpose. Finally, encourage everyone to read the fine print. Continually ask if everyone is happy with every detail of the agreement—better to find out now than later.

4. Escape. As there is no "escape clause" in the contract once it is set, now is the time to get out. There may be people in the group who simply have personal goals that are too extreme to be accommodated in any compromise position (for example, the desire to follow the Spiritual Exercises of Ignatius). If the goal is not negotiable, then they may have to move on and look for another group (or start one). Better for them to leave now, than to stay and agitate or be frustrated. To make this as easy as possible, it is sometimes good to refer to the early group meetings as precontracting. The more exploratory and "unofficial" the process, the less difficult it will be to opt out at any point.

5. Expand. The reverse is also true—people can be drawn in around the formulating contract, contributing their views at the point where they join the process. Naturally, it is easier to add appropriate members once the group has some idea of where it is going.

6. Launch. The great day has arrived—the first official meeting. Before regular activities, start by reviewing the contract one more time. Of course, this is much easier if it is written down (calligraphied scrolls would be a nice touch, but are not necessary!). Some groups like to actually sign one document to seal their commitment—although signing in blood is optional. Celebrate and affirm the whole process in prayer.

7. Regroup. There are many components to a good contract (see the sample below), but a planned time of ending or review is essential. Groups can typically go for 4-6 months on their first contract, and a bit longer on subsequent ones. Simply recalling the purpose and activities of a contract at the end of a cycle can make for a stimulating meeting of evaluation and affirmation. Recontracting can then take place, where the group may deepen commitment in one or more areas, try some new activities or change meeting logistics. This is also the time to say good-by to members moving on to new situations, and to welcome new members (as long as the group is not too old).

There are two variations from this pattern. At the very beginning of a group, contracting can be less than ideal. One or more members (usually the leader) may impose an agenda not generally held, terms may be vaguely defined, someone may withhold a strong desire they had, or an important component of group life may be missed altogether in the discussion (for example, consistent attendance). These deficiencies can produce a lot of frustration which may eventually boil over and therefore require some recontracting after only a few weeks. The other pattern happens near the end of the group's life when the "review" clause is replaced by a "volcano" clause aimed at releasing members into new ministry and new groups.

A Beginning Contract

The following is a sample contract from a real live group:

Who we are at University Chapel

University Chapel is a community of people called to love God and neighbor through celebration and service under the rule of Jesus Christ and the enablement of the Holy Spirit.

Why we exist as a house group

Our purpose in belonging to this house group is:

1. To grow in our understanding of what it means to be a follower of Jesus.

2. To care for and encourage one another in our attempts to follow Jesus and to be his ministers in the world.

What we do

To achieve these goals we intend to do the following both within and outside the context of a weekly meeting:

1. Study the Bible (usually following the University Chapel curriculum, although variation from this may occur if there is a consensus in the group or if a special need arises).

2. Pray for each other.

3. Worship.

4. Have special events (potlucks, book reviews, films, guest speakers, hikes, etc., possibly shared with other house groups).

N.B. Commitment to special projects in the church are appropriate and will be evaluated as they arise.

With regards to the weekly meeting we agree that:

1. We will endeavor to come prepared each evening.

2. We will do our best to be at each meeting.

3. A variety of people will take turns leading the evening meetings.

4. The personal sharing will be kept confidential.

5. The time of gathering will be each Wednesday, 7:15-7:30 p.m., with the meeting to end by 9:30 p.m.

6. We appreciate the need at times for flexibility in the planned agenda and, therefore, will seek to be sensitive to the leading of the Holy Spirit with regards to the direction and subject of discussion.

These goals and objectives will be reviewed early in January.

Resource 2
Group-Size Management

The following is a "weight-watchers" guide for groups trying to keep their size healthy.

Closed-minded

Try this attitude assessment on group size:

1. Is one person's vision dominating the group, pushing for open membership and an overly large group?

2. Is there a fear of the intimacy represented by a smaller group?

3. Are the needs of the many outside the group so much in view that the importance of closed membership for healthy groups is being missed?

4. Is the group deaf to the masses but unable to cope with the request of one friend who wants to join?

5. Is the group willing to consider closed membership and upper limits on membership as separate decisions in a contracting process?

6. Does the group feel that its unspecific contract ("We just want to grow together") gives them no right to limit their membership size?

Just Say No

Here are some tips for turning people down:

Say it impersonally. If it is a friend of a member, let someone other than that member do the talking, preferably outside a group meeting. No new person should be able to just show up at a meeting of a group; that is not the time or place for a conversation about being too full.

Say it nicely. Affirm the person's desire to be in a group. Talk a bit about how groups operate. Try to maintain the person's interest in small groups.

Say it clearly. Make sure the conversation centers on the contract of the group and the importance of group size, so that the person knows that no new member could join at that time. Explain that it is a group decision which was made long before the request.

Say it constructively. Suggest alternative possibilities. If these are not available, light a fire under the program planners. If the group agrees, invite the person to join at the next re-contracting point (assuming that the target size has not been reached yet).

Comings and Goings

No matter how much they ask, new members should not be added when:

1. the group has reached an optimum size (as agreed by the group) or its natural maximum size (as defined by group dynamics).

2. the group's contract would be severely shifted by a whole new agenda introduced with the new members (for example, particularly needy people, seekers, even folks with strong views on prayer and worship).

3. the group is in the middle of a cycle, so that the process of building trust would have to start all over again.

4. the group is more than eighteen months old—even if it has lost some members.

5. the new members would outnumber the old.

6. the group is not healthy.

Resource 3
Leadership-Style Checklist

There are many signs which point to a leadership problem in a group. These signs can be seen even when no direct complaints about the leader have arisen. However, as you consider the following checklist, do not jump to conclusions. It is possible for forces beyond the leader's control to be causing any single phenomenon. On the other hand, if there are more than two checkmarks that emerge in your evaluation of a group, then it is likely that the leadership needs improving.

_____ the leader chairs every meeting

_____ the leader leads every study

_____ in the Bible study, the leader mostly lectures

_____ the leader wants to prepare the study from scratch rather than use a study guide which is available to every member

_____ the group always meets at the leader's house

_____ the leader plays the only instrument used in singing

_____ the leader opens and closes every prayer time

_____ the leader gives a "pastoral prayer" for the whole group at every meeting

_____ the leader shares a lot of personal information

_____ the leader shares very little personal information

_____ the leader seems to be getting burned-out

_____ the leader wants a new leader or a coleader to be assigned

_____ the leader has insisted that the group have open membership

_____ the group is becoming too large

_____ the leader's pet mission project has been adopted by the group

_____ no clear contract has been adopted by the whole group

_____ the leader seems reluctant to talk to the program planners about the group

_____ if you do manage to visit the group, you find a very polite and orderly meeting with members who are especially deferential to the leader

_____ people with strong personalities are leaving the group

_____ the leader is fifteen or more years older than everyone else in the group.

Resource 4
Small Group Coordinator

The work of managing a small group requires a finite list of qualities and skills. The following is a suggested job description.

Overalls:
1. model study and contemplation
2. pray regularly for group members
3. have one particular spiritual friend in the group
4. demonstrate a life-style of witness
5. be prepared, yet teachable
6. know thyself, especially thy limits
7. cultivate a servant heart

Toolbox:
1. bidding—how to contract
2. blueprints—how to plan (weekly, monthly)
3. specification—the four components and the four stages of group life
4. project supervisor—the art of schizophrenia, or observing the group process
5. wrenches and hammers—trouble-shooting specific problems in group dynamics
6. manual—knowing leadership roles and styles
7. plumb line—evaluating the group.

Resource 5
Taming the Over-talkative

The following are some suggestions for dealing with overly-talkative small group members (in increasing order of severity or riskiness).

1. Make sure it is not you that is being over-talkative.

2. Reiterate any agreed-upon ground rules, like "Let's listen to one another," or "Try to reverse your normal pattern and talk less/more."

3. Use careful question directions such as, "I want two people who have not said anything yet to respond," or "I want everyone to answer this one."

4. Use a stopwatch (literally) to set time limits on answers (no one will mind, for everyone will be in the same boat).

5. Sit right beside the talkative person, reducing the eye contact which cues contributions.

6. Interrupt the person in the middle of a long speech and say, "You have made several excellent points—let's see if there is any response to what you have said."

7. Stop looking at the person while he or she is talking—it usually will slow the person down, again because eye cues cease.

8. Expect a mature group to do the work for you, with members humorously and gently reminding the talkative person that he or she is "doing it again." When trust has been built, such communication is possible.

9. Ask the person privately to help draw quieter folks out. (This is a

favorite suggestion in textbooks, but it is dangerous because most talkative people are not dumb—they will know what you are up to—and, besides, quieter folks do not like being drawn out.)

10. Ask the person privately or publicly to shut up (in many ways, the private approach is more risky).

Some of these suggestions may appear to include impolite behavior. But my point is that even interrupting a member is worth it if the health of the group is at stake.

Resource 6
Trouble-shooting Checklist

The following checklist will help you to avoid the doldrums in group life:

Contracting
Did it take place?

Was it thorough enough?

Did everyone contribute?

Was the contract written down?

If some people resisted contracting, is it because they secretly want to get their own way?

Do you have a default contract (the loudest members set the direction without any general agreement)?

Do you have a diluted contract (so vague that no one is challenged and no one knows when the goal has been achieved)?

Stages of Group Life
Are new members constantly joining and catapulting the group back into exploration and transition?

Has the group moved beyond the honeymoon period and begun to be honest about feelings and frustrations?

Are members nervous about sharing more deeply?

How about breaking into smaller units to make sharing easier?

Has confidentiality been discussed?

Is the facilitator modeling vulnerability?

Is he or she too sensitive about the personal threat when members begin to exercise more control in transition?

Do the leaders glory in the leadership roles that others begin to express at this point?

Are the right questions being asked about worship at each stage?

Has mission been alive from the very beginning?

Group Process

Are facilitators being watchful during meetings, noting the sociogram (a picture of who sits where, and who talks to who, and for how long) or keeping track of the roles people play?

Do they feel free to share this information openly with the group so that every member becomes aware of the dynamics going on?

Are they helping people to fight fair, not allowing any ganging up on one member, or constant accusations rather than expressions of hurt?

Do they try to subvert groupthink? (By "groupthink" I mean the negative process of groups coming to a false consensus, where seniority, enthusiasm or a desire for unity crowds out dissenting opinion.)

Planning

Are meetings carefully planned, but with spontaneous times built in?

Is a journal of meetings kept, so that ruts can be avoided? (For example, do you always open with the same sharing question?)

Are meetings evaluated regularly, and followed by attempts to improve?

Progress

Is the overall life of a group reviewed at the end of a contract, with a concerted effort to devise a more challenging contract for the next round? (For example, after six months together, the members might want to establish a deeper level of accountability around spiritual disciplines and start prayer partnerships.)

Beyond the Meeting

Are facilitators encouraging social contacts and events outside the formal meeting?

Are some meetings canceled altogether in favor of a fun event?

Are facilitators seeing or at least calling individual members from time to time?

Are members encouraged to do this as well?

Resource 7
Models for Mission Groups

The following are some possible models for mission groups:

Multiple Focus Support Group. This is where people with different mission interests (usually within one broad type of mission) band together for prayer, wisdom and some practical support.

An example would be the Social Justice Group which ran for several years at a church I attended. The strength of this group was the emotional and spiritual support it afforded to those active in the world of social justice—a world which can be very lonely for evangelicals who are met with suspicion from both the more conservative members of their home church and the more liberal leaders of the "justice community." The weakness of the group was that the hodge-podge of concerns, from nuclear arms proliferation to environmental problems to feminist issues, made for a stimulating but ultimately frustrating time. Efforts were too dissipated to create any sense of concerted impact on any one area. In my current church, some of the same people have begun to focus more, taking on one educational goal each year in the wider church community, and beginning to develop single projects to tackle together.

Single Focus Support Group. This is similar to the previous type in that the mission mainly happens through the members working individually outside the group, but different because the mission of each person is the same.

An example here would be an evangelism training group. I ran several of these as an InterVarsity staffworker on a university campus. It was a very simple strategy, operating under the banner of the Lifestyle Evangelism Project (LEP). I met with two or three students for several weeks in a cafeteria to teach some basic concepts about witnessing. Between meetings each of us would pray for opportunities to put the principle just learned into practice. Some of these students would then go on to lead their own LEP groups. God richly blessed this little program, and I still believe it could find a home in many churches.

The advantages over the first type of mission group are clear: more possibility for meaningful training, more useful encouragement and exhortation (because everyone is sharing the same experience), and a greater sense of accomplishment as a group. Other types of groups which would fall under this heading are occupational support networks (members of your church in the arts, teaching, business, law, and so on), and parenting support groups.

Limited-Project Action Group. Some mission groups move beyond the previous types, where the mission is happening primarily through individual members, to embrace a project that requires more teamwork. Such groups may be further subdivided into those working on projects limited in some way, as opposed to those with a more open-ended agenda. The former mission projects may be limited in scope, in the regularity of obligation, or in duration.

Some of these projects are accomplished mainly within the confines of the group meeting. I identify these as *in camera* groups, meaning "not in public." They would include various kinds of intercessory prayer groups, as well as outreach Bible studies. (See IVP's booklet *How to Begin an Evangelistic Bible Study.*) Therapy groups would also fit into this category, plus groups aimed at incorporating newcomers in your church.

Other groups with closely circumscribed projects do their planning within the meeting, but perform the mission mainly outside official meeting times. For these I coin the term *ex camera*. Here one might include the Drama Group I led in Intervarsity. We would rehearse (as well as do Bible study, pray, and so on) during our meetings, and then make presentations (literally perform our mission) in various public gatherings.

Another candidate for this category would be the "6:30 at 630" group in our church. This group got its name from the mission that had brought it together, namely to host a social one Friday a month at 6:30 p.m. at a house with the address 630. The members of this group really knew how to do public relations and how to party!

A ministry I heard about at a church in Ohio would also fit here. They formed "compassion teams" comprised of three laypersons to provide paraprofessional care for people with complex problems. For example, a team might be attached to an older woman who has just been widowed. It could include a grief and depression specialist, a household fix-it type, and a spiritual friend. They would meet on an ad hoc basis for prayer and consultation, with most of their ministry happening "outside" the group with the widow herself.

Extended-Project Action Group. The final major category includes groups whose purpose might be quite defined in focus but very open-ended in terms of strategy, time and energy.

This would include almost every mission group begun at the Church of the Savior in Washington, D.C. (coffeehouse ministries, housing projects, literacy programs—see Gordon Cosby's *Handbook for Mission Groups*). The category also includes the aborted eastside mission described at the beginning of this chapter, as well as the more successful community-building group I have been involved with recently, a group charged with the responsibility for developing the groups program in our church. Other examples would be neighbors' prayer groups, groups reaching out in a particular workplace, worship ensembles, youth ministry teams, and church-planting cells.

Naturally, other kinds of categories could be employed (such as one based on the expected duration of the group). Or the above categories could be further refined (the "in camera" groups could be broken down into open and closed membership groups—with drop-in seeker studies fitting into the first type—and the "ex camera" groups could be broken down into those working inside the church and those working outside).

Resource 8
Choosing a Bible Study Guide

There are a number of guidelines that are useful in choosing between the dozens of Bible study guides available. I offer the criteria here rather than listing my favorite publishers because (1) I do not want to introduce only my personal bias, (2) not all guides in a published series are equally good, and (3) I am not necessarily aware of all the good guides out there (for example, the one you are writing yourself). So consult the following checklist when you peruse the study guide department in your local bookstore.

What to Look For

1. Attractive cover. Can you tell a book by its cover? Surprisingly often you can. Care in the packaging is a sign of careful editing. Besides, a little beauty never hurts.

2. Brief introductions to the concept and practice of group Bible study, and to the particular book or topic under consideration. A study chapter with questions overviewing the whole biblical book is a nice touch.

3. Table of contents and page numbers, to help people plan ahead and navigate from week-to-week.

4. Catchy chapter titles, and engaging, brief (no more than ten line) introductions to each chapter which relate as much to contemporary issues, felt needs, and the purpose of the study as to biblical background

or context.

5. Division of the biblical book or topic into appropriately bite-sized pieces. A paragraph of Paul in the hand is often worth two Old Testament chapters in the bush (unless it is a burning bush). You know what I mean.

6. An attempt to hit the high points (for example, lots of skimming to pick out key themes) where large passages are being tackled. Reading (especially with long passages) should be active, linked to an observational goal (for example, "Read verses 1-10, noticing the mood of the characters").

7. No more than twelve suggested questions, mostly crisp and concise in wording.

8. A good balance between the three types of inductive questions: observation, interpretation and application. My rule of thumb for proportions: 2:3:1.

9. A hook or approach question to start out the study which gets the student or group thinking about their own life before they even think about the text. 10. References to the verses to which questions relate (rather than keeping them guessing), though some questions should be less directed.

11. A simple, eye-pleasing layout, with enough room to write in answers (I like blank space rather than lines for writing, but this is more a matter of taste).

12. Some brief background notes built into the chapter. If the notes are longer, they should be limited to an appendix.

What to Avoid

1. Lots and lots of text at any point. I am afraid that the judgement is in—this is an anti-reading age.

2. Division of the material into overly small sections so that natural thematic units are disrupted or the pace of progress is slow to the point of discouragement (I have rarely encountered this problem in published

guides, but you never know).

3. Being asked to read too much of a long passage before answering some questions. It is also bad to divide the reading and questions into sections but never relate the sections together in some kind of summary of the main point.

4. The purpose or aim of the study is not stated or implicitly obvious as one moves through the questions. All you get is a series of disconnected ideas that came to the author as they studied the passage.

Note that the purpose is not the same as a topic, such as "love of enemies." A purpose relates a goal of personal transformation to the main truth gleaned from the passage—"to learn how and why we should love our enemies." This represents a cognitive change. Even better are goals of attitude or behavior change—"to identify an enemy in our lives and plan one way to love them in the next month in the manner which Jesus teaches."

5. The "trick" of including supplementary or multiple questions under one number in the guide. This is not only confusing, it leads to an excessive number of questions. In one study I surveyed, there were sixteen question numbers (already a problem), but actually 34 questions, and 11 other directions such as "note" or "compare" for the poor group to follow in one sitting! Also, be wary of guides that provide too many options, "for further study" items or sections headed "as time allows"—these just product guilt.

6. Too much attention to self-disclosure, community-building or personal opinions and not enough time looking at the Bible.

7. Too many leading questions requiring only "yes" or "no" or fill-in-the-blank answers or, at the other extreme, loaded questions requiring long dissertations.

8. Too many directions with vague goals, leading the student to ask "So what?" and become discouraged with work that does not pay off. Examples include "compare," "contrast" or "list."

9. Too many trite observations questions (for example, "Who is speaking in v. 7?"). Simple facts should just be assumed in the way questions are asked. On the other hand, another problem is complex interpretation questions with inadequate groundwork in the text laid down.

10. Absent application questions, or only global ones, focusing, for example, on the whole church, rather than personal change.

11. Too many background helps such as, charts, maps, and Greek word studies that give details unnecessary to the purpose, or which steer the student towards the author's interpretative grid rather than towards self-discovery in the biblical text. Sometimes theories of literary structure or vocabulary usage are less important than the simple message of the story or exposition.

12. Lop-sided selection of focal chapters from a long book or verses from a long passage. Although selectivity is always necessary, the main points should not be missed. The worst case I ever encountered was a guide on Romans which left out chapters 9—11 because they were too difficult!

Split Decision

There are a half-dozen features of study guides about which I am neutral. Sometimes these features are good, sometimes they are detrimental.

1. Cartoons, graphics and fun exercises. As this book shows, I like cartoons. But there are problems with including such items in a guide. It requires a lot of creativity to make them fit a study purpose rather than being added on for their own sake. Sometimes they are good, but they still distract from Bible study itself. Even in the best cases, some people simply do not like fun stuff, especially when they give a "youth group" feel to the guide.

2. Quotations. The drawbacks just described for comic relief features apply here too, with one difference—commentary from experts make the guide appear too intellectual rather than too juvenile.

3. Biblical text provided. I like this in some ways. It eliminates the complication of comparing different Bible versions. However, there is one main problem: some people (or whole churches) only want to use their own version and resist changing to another. Now, if the version happens to be the one generally used in your organization, or if the guide is taken by each member to the group meeting (which, in fact, I do not recommend), then such study guides might be convenient and useful. On the other hand, comparing different versions is also very instructive sometimes.

4. Reviewing previous chapters. Actually, this is a good thing *as long as time is allowed for it.* It is not good when, as I often see, it is included in the final question in the study guide. Furthermore, clear directions to manage the review should be given. A good example is "Find the main application you want to take away from this series and share it with the group."

5. Explanatory comments on each question. Again, I like these up to a point—as long as they do not provide the "correct" answer to the question and cut-off a sense of open-ended discovery. Sometimes it is all right to provide in an appendix a summary of different historical perspectives on a passage or other helps for the study leader, as long as the study guide is not turned into a mini-commentary with too much detail.

6. Fill-in charts. Occasionally these are okay, but no one format should be overused. As well, fill-in charts are sometimes another way of asking for uninterpreted work, similar to "compare" or "list" exercises. Finally, charts are sometimes so structured, with nice alliterative subheadings, that they impose the author's personal analysis rather than provide an opportunity for discovery on the part of the student.

Miscellaneous Tips

It will already be clear from the previous section that no published study guide is perfect, and that some types might be better for certain groups than others. Guides with a lot of diversions are good for most youth studies. Guides with fill-in exercises can be a good introduction for people new to the Bible (or new to reading), and guides with a lot of detailed notes or analysis can be good for advanced, dig-in studies.

One important truth should not be forgotten: No matter what the background of the student—young or old, educated or not, believer or seeker—all study guides should promote independent observation, contemplation and application of the actual biblical text. After preparing for the study, group members should leave the guide at home (or sit on it) so that the study leader can follow a plan inspired by their preparation and the particular needs of the group.

When you chose a guide, you might get members to pay for their own copies in order to increase a sense of ownership (and commitment to do nomework). One exception might be outreach studies, where materials are provided free to seekers (though they, like anyone, value what they pay for).

The Most Excellent Way

Almost any kind of published guide can serve as some kind of a resource for a leader who is preparing a study. However, the best kind of all is the guide written and printed by your church itself (which is more realistic than the absolute ideal of individual leaders preparing totally from scratch). Although self-publishing takes a lot of work, there are several advantages to this approach (as outlined by Paul Stevens, "Honing the Two-Edged Sword," *Leadership 100,* Nov.-Dec. 1983, pp. 12-15).

The main advantage is that you can select purposes that fit the goals of your organization, and structure the material to fit different agendas. For example, you might include family material, group exercises, questions for spiritual friends, and even the church budget!

One goal in my home church has been to limit the biblical data to which people get exposed during any one week in order to maximize the potential for obedience. Therefore, we have not minded the absence of an evening service, mid-week prayer meeting or adult Sunday school. Furthermore, we have consistently provided curriculum for personal and group study that dovetails with the Sunday teaching (generally used *before* the plenary teaching). Basically, one biblical text alone shapes the adult learning and, recently, the ministry to children each week (though groups are given the freedom to study other material if they want).

There are two cautions I would add about writing your own guides. First, be sure to follow the same checklist of quality criteria outlined above. And, second, be sure to still leave your guide at home when you go to the meeting, giving the leader a chance to follow his or her own plan.

Further Reading

Cosby, Gordon. *Handbook for Mission Groups.* Washington, D.C.: Church of the Savior. Reprint available from Fuller Seminary Bookstore, 135 N. Oakland Ave., Pasadena, Calif. 91101.

Although dated, there is wonderful inspiration and instruction here for all manner of mission groups. If you can find it, there is little else to match the credibility of this manual.

Griffin, Em. *Getting Together.* Downers Grove, Ill.: InterVarsity Press, 1982.

Worth reading for the cartoons and the chapter on deviance alone, this is a great textbook on the community component of group life.

Hestenes, Roberta. *Using the Bible in Groups.* Philadelphia, Penn.: Westminster, 1985.

Do not be put off by the cover or the title! It covers more than just Bible study. Along with an outline of twenty different study methods, it includes positive material on group dynamics which complements the principles in this book.

Lum, Ada. *How to Begin an Evangelistic Bible Study.* Downers Grove, Ill.: InterVarsity Press, 1971.

A classic outline of the why's and how's of one popular mission group type.

Nicholas, Ron, et al. *Good Things Come in Small Groups.* Downers Grove, Ill.: InterVarsity Press, 1985.

This is the best popular introduction to small group life, including a good outline of group dynamics and great resources for the four components of a balanced group (nurture, community, worship and mission). It also includes one of the few chapters around on running a small group program.

Nyquist, James F., and Jack Kuhatschek. *Leading Bible Discussions.* Downers Grove, Ill.: InterVarsity Press, 1985.

The best brief introduction to inductive Bible study and discussion dynamics.

Peace, Richard. *Small Group Evangelism.* Downers Grove, Ill.: InterVarsity Press, 1985.

A comprehensive primer for groups that want to focus intensively on personal evangelism for one contract cycle.

You will have noted the heavy InterVarsity Press emphasis in this list. Unfortunately, the new NavPress materials did not get to me in time to review.